RWBY

RWBY

MARGUERITE BENNETT
writer

MIRKA ANDOLFO
MEGHAN HETRICK
GABRIELE BAGNOLI
artists

ARIF PRIANTO
colorist

GABRIELA DOWNIE
letterer

SARAH STONE
collection cover artist

ANDREW MARINO Editor – Original Series
JEB WOODARD Group Editor – Collected Editions
SCOTT NYBAKKEN Editor – Collected Edition
STEVE COOK Design Director – Books
GABRIEL MALDONADO Publication Design
DANIELLE DIGRADO Publication Production

BOB HARRAS Senior VP – Editor-in-Chief, DC Comics

DAN DiDIO Publisher
JIM LEE Publisher & Chief Creative Officer
BOBBIE CHASE VP – New Publishing Initiatives
DON FALLETTI VP – Manufacturing Operations & Workflow Management
LAWRENCE GANEM VP – Talent Services
ALISON GILL Senior VP – Manufacturing & Operations
HANK KANALZ Senior VP – Publishing Strategy & Support Services
DAN MIRON VP – Publishing Operations
NICK J. NAPOLITANO VP – Manufacturing Administration & Design
NANCY SPEARS VP – Sales
JONAH WEILAND VP – Marketing & Creative Services
MICHELE R. WELLS VP & Executive Editor, Young Reader

RWBY

DC Comics, 2900 West Alameda Ave., Burbank, CA 91505
Printed by LSC Communications, Kendallville, IN, USA. 7/3/20. First Printing.
ISBN: 978-1-77950-301-5

Library of Congress Cataloging-in-Publication Data is available.

PEFC Certified
This product is from sustainably managed forests and controlled sources
PEFC
PEFC/29-31-337
www.pefc.org

JIM
LEE

THEN.
I LOVE STORIES.
THAT'S WHAT EVERYONE THOUGHT I'D BE, WHEN I WAS A LITTLE KID--
"RUBY ROSE, YOU WERE BORN TO BE A *STORYTELLER.*"
I LOVED THE SONGS, THE FIGHTS, THE BATTLES, THE ROMANCES.
THEN THERE CAME A DAY WHEN I REALIZED...
...I DIDN'T HAVE TO JUST TELL THE STORIES.
LATER.
I COULD LIVE MY OWN.
Prologue:
The Elegy
Marguerite Bennett Writer
Mirka Andolfo Artist Arif Prianto Colorist
Gabriela Downie Letterer Sarah Stone Cover
Jim Lee and Alex Sinclair Variant Cover
Andrew Marino Editor

OUR WORLD HAS BEEN THREATENED, FOR AS LONG AS ANYONE CAN REMEMBER, BY THESE CREATURES, MONSTERS, CALLED GRIMM.
NO ONE KNOWS WHERE THEY CAME FROM, BUT THE PEOPLE WHO FIGHT THEM, WHO FIGHT TO SAVE THE WHOLE WORLD OF REMNANT--
--ARE CALLED HUNTSMEN.
ATLAS, VALE, VACUO, AND MISTRAL--EVERY KINGDOM IN REMNANT HAS THEIR OWN WAY OF DEALING WITH GRIMM.
BUT ONLY THE KINGDOM OF VALE HAS BEACON--
--THE LEGENDARY ACADEMY, WHERE MY MOTHER AND FATHER WENT TO BECOME HUNTSMEN.
AND THAT'S WHAT I WANTED TO BE.
I WANTED TO HELP PEOPLE, HUNT MONSTERS--
--AND FIGHT ALONGSIDE MY FAMILY.

BUT SOME THINGS... DON'T ALWAYS GO THE WAY YOU DREAM.
AND SOME DREAMS...
...REALLY DO COME TRUE.
COME ON, MS. "I GOT SPECIAL PERMISSION TO ENTER BEACON ACADEMY TWO YEARS EARLY BY ORDER OF PROFESSOR OZPIN"!
YOU'RE GONNA BE LATE FOR CLASS!
I WAS SO GLAD I HAD MY SISTER THERE.
I NEVER KNEW WHAT FRIENDS I HAD, UNTIL BEACON.

MY SISTER'S NAME IS YANG XIAO LONG.
IT'S COMPLETELY UNDERSTANDABLE IF YOU HAVE A CRUSH ON HER.
YOU HAVEN'T HEARD HER SNORE YET.
SHE'S A BALLER, BRAWLER, BUTTKICK SCHOLAR, MY SISTER-FROM-A-DIFFERENT-MISTER-EXCEPT-NOT-A-MISTER-BECAUSE-WE-DO-ACTUALLY-HAVE-DIFFERENT-MOMS-BUT-THE-SAME-DAD.
AND THIS IS BLAKE BELLADONNA!
YOU KNOW THAT SKITTISH, SKINNY ALLEY CAT YOU KEEP TRYING TO FEED BUT YOU'RE ALSO PROBABLY PRETTY SURE THE CAT IS SMART AND STREETWISE ENOUGH TO GET ITS OWN MILK AND IT'S JUST KIND OF INDULGING YOU BECAUSE IT KNOWS IT WOULD REALLY, REALLY MEAN A LOT TO YOU TO BE ABLE TO PET A CAT THIS STYLISH AND COOL?
THAT'S BLAKE
AND YOU KNOW THAT FLUFFY, SNUB-NOSED, PAMPERED WHITE CAT THAT SLEEPS IN A HUGE, BEAUTIFUL, FRILLY BED AND HAS A BUNCH OF SERVANTS TO BRING IT PÂTÉ AND CHICKEN LIVERS AND FRESH FISH AND IS 100 PERCENT SPOILED AND CODDLED AND BABIED AND USELESS?
OKAY, THAT'S NOT REMOTELY WEISS, BECAUSE WEISS SCHNEE?
SHE WORKS INCREDIBLY, RIDICULOUSLY HARD.
YOU SHOULD SEE HER GRADES!
THEY HAVE TO KEEP COMING UP WITH, LIKE, PLATINUM AND PALLADIUM AND OSMIUM MEDALS BECAUSE GOLD DOESN'T EVEN CUT IT ANYMORE!

WE COME FROM DIFFERENT PLACES, DIFFERENT FAMILIES, DIFFERENT CONTINENTS, DIFFERENT KINGDOMS.
BUT WE ALL WANTED THIS.
TO BE BETTER. TO BE HUNTRESSES.
AND TOGETHER--
--WE'RE
TEAM RWBY.

ALL THE TEAMS ARE NAMED FOR COLORS-- AND ALMOST ALL OF US ARE, TOO.
ART USED TO BE OUTLAWED, AND I THINK IT'S A KIND OF REMINDER.
NO MATTER HOW BLEAK, DARK, AND SIGHTLESS THE WORLD BECOMES, WE'RE STILL HERE.
LIFE AND BEAUTY AND COLOR AND STORIES ARE STILL HERE.
WE'LL COME BACK. WE'LL GO ON.
THAT POWER IS WHAT WE CALL A SEMBLANCE.
MY SEMBLANCE IS AN ICE CREAM SUNDAE OF SPEED WITH A LITTLE CHERRY OF TELEPORTATION ON TOP.
WEISS CAN SUMMON ANY GRIMM SHE'S SLAIN.
YANG CAN WALLOP BACK WITH ALL THE ENERGY SHE'S ABSORBED FROM A BLOW.

HAT'S WHAT BEACON ACADEMY REPRESENTS, IN A
Y--HOW CLOSE ALL OF REMNANT CAME TO THE END,
AND THEN HOW IT FOUGHT BACK THAT DARKNESS.
AT BEACON, WE LEARN ABOUT COMBAT, AND DUST, WHICH IS OUR BIGGEST SOURCE OF ENERGY--
--AND, HEHE, YEAH...
...WE LEARN ABOUT OUR POWERS.
FOR STARTERS-- EVERY LIVING THING HAS A SOUL.
YOUR SOUL IS WHAT GIVES YOU YOUR AURA, AND THAT AURA LETS YOU DO SOMETHING NO OTHER PERSON CAN DO.
SOMETHING THAT MAKES YOU SPECIAL OUT OF ALL THE PEOPLE IN THE WORLD--WHETHER HUMAN OR FAUNUS, OR ANYTHING ELSE BESIDES.
AND BLAKE CAN MAKE SHADOW-CLONES OF HERSELF, ALL TO DISTRACT HER ENEMY SO SHE CAN DISAPPEAR!
BETWEEN AURAS, SEMBLANCES, DUST WEAPONS, AND COMBAT, IT'S A LOT TO REMEMBER.
AND RECENTLY, I'VE BEEN HEARING SOME WEIRD, WHISPERED RUMORS...
...SOMETHING ABOUT "THE MYTH OF THE FOUR MAIDENS," AND...MAGIC.
BUT THAT'S JUST A FAIRY TALE, RIGHT?
EVERYONE KNOWS THERE'S NO SUCH THING AS MAGIC.
BUT THIS IS WHAT WE WERE ALL GOING TO BE--
--HUNTRESSES.
HEROES OF BEACON.
WEISS, AND BLAKE, AND YANG, AND ME.
TEAM RWBY

THE BATTLE OF BEACON ACADEMY.
BUT NONE OF IT TURNED OUT THAT WAY.
A SPLINTER GROUP CALLED THE WHITE FANG BROKE INTO BEACON.
GRIMM WERE UNLEASHED UPON THE SCHOOL.
AND SOME OF MY FRIENDS...
...THEY DIDN'T MAKE IT.

THE ISLAND OF PATCH.
IN THE AFTERMATH AND ALL THE DAYS GONE BY, I CAME BACK TO MY DAD'S HOUSE.
RUBY!
THE HARBOR OF VALE.
BLAKE HAD RUN FOR IT.
THE HELIPAD OF BEACON.
WEISS'S FAMILY DRAGGED HER HOME.
THE HOME OF TAIYANG.
AND YANG...YANG WAS RECOVERING.

THE ISLAND OF PATCH. NOW.
OUT OF OUR BROKEN TEAMS, THE SURVIVORS OF BEACON MADE SOMETHING NEW.
JAUNE, NORA, REN, AND I NEED TO FIND OUT WHO SENT THE WHITE FANG TO ATTACK BEACON--AND WHY.
BUT WITH MY FRIENDS SCATTERED AND GONE--
--WHAT HAPPENS NOW?
THE HOME OF TAIYANG.
NO MATTER HOW BLEAK AND DARK AND SIGHTLESS THE WORLD BECOMES, WE'RE STILL HERE.
THE SCHNEE FAMILY MANOR.
LIFE AND BEAUTY AND COLOR AND STORIES ARE STILL HERE.
THE SEA OF MENAGERI
WE'LL COME BACK.
WE'LL GO ON.
...WON'T WE?

HE FOREST
OF HINOKI.
THE CONTINENT
OF ANIMA.
JUST A FEW HUNDRED MILES TO MISTRAL, JUST A FEW HUNDRED MORE TO GO! WHO ATTACKED BEACON?
WHAT WERE THEY AFTER? THAT'S WHAT WE WANT TO KNOW!
YOU OKAY, RUBY?
YOU SOUND MOST UN-RUBY-ISHLY QUIET.
WE'RE ONLY A FEW DAYS OUT OF PATCH. THIS IS NO TIME TO FLAG IN OUR MORALE!
TEAM RNJR DOES NOT NEED A FLAG.
YOU--YOU DON'T THINK YANG IS MAD AT YOU FOR GOING, DO YOU?
I...
...I THINK...
...IN HER VERY TRUEST HEART...
...YANG WOULD BE MAD IF I DIDN'T GO.
SHE'S HURTING RIGHT NOW. AND SOME-TIMES... SHE CAN BE CLUMSY.
BUT YANG... HAS NEVER HAD TROUBLE KNOWING WHAT'S RIGHT.
HEY, MUST BE A FAMILY TRAIT.
HEH. MAYBE.
MY MOM WAS A HERO.
AND WELL, I'M PRETTY SURE MOST MOMS ARE.

THE ISLAND OF PATCH.
THEN.
R BUT THERE ARE A LOT OF MOMS...
...AND SUMMER ROSE IS MINE.
OR... UH...WAS MINE, I GUESS.
NO. STILL IS MINE!
EVEN THOUGH...
IN MEMORY
RUBY: PART 1
STORIES
Marguerite Bennett Writer
Mirka Andolfo Artist Arif Prianto Colorist
Gabriela Downie Letterer Andrew Marino Editor
IT'S ALMOST HER BIRTHDAY. WE STILL HAVE CAKE.
BUT MY DAD...
HIS FRIENDS...
RIGHT NOW NOBODY WILL TALK TO ME ABOUT HER.
MAYBE THEY'RE SAD, OR--

HUGS FROM ABOVE!
YAAAANG!
WHY'S BABY SISTER BLUE?
DAD AND HIS FRIENDS-- THEY'RE ALL TOO BUSY WITH GROWN-UP STUFF...
...GETTING READY FOR MOM'S BIRTHDAY PARTY, EVEN THOUGH SHE'S GONE.
I JUST WANT TO HEAR STORIES ABOUT HER.
AW, I CAN HELP! YOU WANT STORIES ABOUT SUMMER ROSE?
SHE WAS MY MOM, TOO, YOU KNOW, NO MATTER WHAT DAD'S NEIGHBORS SAY ABOUT "HALF-" OR "STEP-" OR WHATEVER--
SO, RUBY ROSE, LET ME TELL YOU THE BALLAD OF THE HERO OF BEACON--
POTATOES
TOMATOES
HERBS
--THE HUNTRESS SUMMER ROSE!
ONCE, SUMMER ROSE RESCUED A PRINCESS FROM A TOWER HIIIIIGH IN THE MOUNTAINS!
SHE HAD TO USE HER SWORD TO GET THROUGH A WHOLE MAZE TO DO IT, AND SUMMER ROSE SOLVED IT IN, LIKE, A MINUTE!
AND THEN ANOTHER TIME, SUMMER ROSE KILLED THE BIGGEST GRIMM EVER!
IT WAS A BILLION FEET TALL! IT WAS, LIKE, AS BIG AS A BUILDING!
IT WAS TALLER THAN DAD!
SUMMER ROSE EVEN COOKED A HUUUUUGE FEAST FOR A KING AND ALL HIS KNIGHTS. GUY KNIGHTS AND LADY KNIGHTS, AND HUMAN KNIGHTS AND FAUNUS KNIGHTS--
--SHE MADE EVERYTHING OUT OF COOKIES! COOKIE STEAK! COOKIE DUMPLINGS! COOKIE CAKE! COOKIE PLATES AND COOKIE SILVERWARE!
COOKIE CHANDELIERS!

AND THAT'S THE TRUTH!
NOW YOU GO AND PLAY, RUBY! I HAVE TO HELP DAD SET THE TABLE BEFORE ALL THE GUESTS GET HERE!
WOW... MY MOM REALLY WAS THE HERO OF BEACON...
HEY, LITTLE BLACK BIRD!
DO YOU WANT TO HEAR A STORY ABOUT MY MOM?
I KNOW LOTS NOW, AND--
YOU DON'T KNOW LOTS, LITTLE GIRL.
YOU KNOW LIES.
UHH... WHAT?! HOW'RE YOU TALKING?!
YOU TRULY BELIEVED ALL THAT FOLDEROL ABOUT WHAT A MAGNIFICENT, PERFECT WIFE AND HUNTRESS YOUR MOTHER WAS?
TCH.
YANG ISN'T SUMMER ROSE'S DAUGHTER.
SUMMER ROSE COULD NEVER BE A TRUE MOTHER TO YANG.
SHE WAS WEAK--
--AND NO CHILD OF HERS COULD BE BETTER.
S-S-STOP--!
YOU'RE LYING!
YOU'RE-- YOU'RE--

THE FOREST OF HINOKI.
NOW.
GRIMM!
W-WEAPONS UP!
JAUNE! LANCERS ON YOUR RIGHT!
RUBY--
--IN YOUR BLIND SPOT!
BEHIND YOU--!

THEN.
THWCK
CAW
CAW
CAW
YOU'RE A GRIMM!
NOOOO! NOOO...
RUBY!
BABY SISTER, WHAT'S WRONG?!
SNIFFLE
WERE... WERE THE STORIES YOU TOLD ME...
...WERE THEY TRUE, YANG?
...
BWAAAAAAAAWWW!
HEY, HEY!
WHAT IS THIS? ARE YOU TRYING TO PUT THE ROOSTERS OUT OF A JOB?!
UNCLE QROW!
OOOF!
UNCLE QROW!
WHUMPH
COFF
KOFF

A RAVEN, YOU SAY?
AND VERY INTERESTED IN TELLING YOU SUMMER ROSE WASN'T A GREAT MOTHER, ESPECIALLY TO YANG...
HMM.
YANG. YOU SHOULDN'T HAVE TOLD RUBY THOSE STORIES. EVEN IF YOU MEANT THEM KINDLY.
YOUR FATHER AND I DISAGREE ON THIS, BUT A LIE IS A LIE, AS FAR AS I'M CONCERNED.
AND, RUBY, YOU'RE A BIG GIRL NOW. BIG GIRLS DO NOT LOSE THEIR TEMPER EVERY TIME A BIRD INSULTS THEIR MOTHER.
THAT IS A VERY FAMOUS PROVERB AND I'M SURPRISED YOU HAVEN'T HEARD IT BEFORE NOW.
BUT. IF YOU WANT THE TRUTH.
MAYBE I CAN HELP YOU.
U-UNCLE QROW?
YOUR MOTHER DIDN'T USE A SWORD LIKE YANG TOLD YOU.
=SNORT= BUT THEN, I DON'T THINK I'LL SHOW YOU WHAT WEAPON SHE ACTUALLY USED.
THESE WILL BE A GOOD ENOUGH START.

"SUMMER ROSE USED HER ENEMIES' EGOS AGAINST THEM--
"THEY SAW THIS LITTLE WAIF AND UNDERESTIMATED HER, BUT SHE WAS RELENTLESS, EVERY TIME.
"SHE WAS ALWAYS THE FIRST TO HELP, THOUGH.
"FIRST TO VOLUNTEER ON A SEARCH AND RESCUE. FIRST TO DIVVY UP AND SHARE RATIONS, WHEN WE GOT STRANDED ON A MISSION--
"--SHE AND I GOT INTO A TERRIBLE FIGHT ABOUT THAT. I THOUGHT TAIYANG WAS GOING TO BREAK MY NOSE.
"SHE WASN'T PERFECT.
"SOMETIMES SHE FALTERED.
"SHE DIDN'T KNOW WHO SHE WAS UNLESS SHE WAS HELPING OTHER PEOPLE, AND LET ME TELL YOU...

"SHE COULD BE DECEIVED, THOUGH.
"SHE STOPPED TO HELP A BEGGAR IN VALE, AND HE WOUND UP ROBBING HER BLIND.
"RAVEN HAD TO COME AND BAIL HER OUT.
"...IT IS TERRIBLE NOT TO KNOW WHO YOU ARE UNLESS YOU'RE DEFINED BY OTHER PEOPLE.
"BUT SHE WAS KIND, AND SHE WAS STRONG, AND SHE WAS BRAVE, AND SHE--
"--SHE LOVED YOU BOTH.
"MORE THAN I THINK YOU CAN EVEN IMAGINE."

SO.
DO YOU WANT YOUR FIRST FIGHTING LESSON?
NEVER-- LET-- THE-- ENEMY-- GET-- INSIDE-- YOUR-- HEAD.
DON'T WIN THAT BATTLE FOR THEM. NOW COME ON.
NEXT LESSON WILL BE TONIGHT, AFTER CAKE.
DO YOU THINK WE'LL DO GOOD, UNCLE QROW?
AS GOOD AS SUMMER ROSE?
HEH. NO.
BUT ONE DAY...
Q "...I WOULDN'T BE SURPRISED."
NEXT: YANG'S RECOVERY!

THE HOME OF TAIYANG.
THE ISLAND OF PATCH.
WHY ARE YOU ANGRY, YANG?
I'M NOT ANGRY.
ASHAMED?
NOT ASHAMED.
GUILTY?
NO.
The Man With Two Souls
With
YOU MIGHT LIKE IT.
A DANCE?
YANG!
JUST SAD.
FLING

THAT BAD, HUH?
WHAT HAPPENED-- DID THE DOG DIE?
...
THAT'S OKAY.
I JUST CAME TO TELL YOU THERE'S AN OLD LADY IN THE VILLAGE, MADAME MALLARI, WHO NEEDS SOME CHORES DONE.
YOU'VE BEEN CONSCRIPTED, MISSY.
DON'T, DAD. JUST DON'T.
HEY, I'M NOT IN CHARGE OF IT. TAKE IT UP WITH HER IF YOU WANT.
I KNOW WHAT THIS IS.
AND I DON'T WANT CHARITY.
THEN PROVE IT.
GO DOWN THERE AND SHOW HER.
FINE!
I WILL!

MADAME MALLARI?
GOOD AFTERNOON, YANG!
THANK YOU SO KINDLY FOR YOUR AID. I'VE REALLY BEEN IGNORING THESE PROBLEMS FOR TOO LONG, AND TODAY, AS THEY SAY, THE BANDAGE IS COMING OFF--
Yang: Part 1
Rebuilding
Marguerite Bennett Writer Mirka Andolfo Artist
Arif Prianto Colorist Gabriela Downie Letterer
Sarah Stone Cover Stanley "Artgerm" Lau Variant Cover
Andrew Marino Editor
I'VE A HOLLOW TREE THAT NEEDS UP-ROOTING--
--FIELDS THAT HAVE BEEN JUST ABOUT SUCKED DRY OF DECENT SOIL--
--A ROTTEN TROUGH THAT NEEDS REPLACING--
--AND A FILTHY BARN THAT STINKS LIKE--WELL, I'M SURE YOU CAN IMAGINE AN ABSOLUTELY REVOLTING SIMILE.
?

BANG
OH GRAPES!
HERBS, POTIONS, DUST, GLYPHS...
MADAME MALLARI IS A HEALER...A HEALER, LIKE...
...BIG-TIME.
SHE...
IF I...
COULD SHE...?
YANG, DON'T DO IT.
DON'T GET YOUR HOPES UP.
...YOU ALSO GO TO A MONSTER-HUNTING SCHOOL AND YOUR SOUL GIVES YOU SUPER-POWERS.
MAYBE KEEP AN OPEN MIND.
AND WHAT IF THIS IS WHY DAD SENT ME HERE...

OKAY, COME ON, BIG GUY, RIGHT IN CENTER MASS--
BOO.
OOF
YEAAAAAH, BUDDY!
TEN POINTS!
THAR SHE BLOWS!
WHSSSSSSSH

AND AS FOR FERTILIZER--
--WELL, NO ONE EVER SAID GROWTH WAS PLEASANT.
AND NOW FOR THE FUN PART--
HIIII-YAH!!
WHUMPH
AND A LITTLE OFF THE TOP--
HECK YEAH.

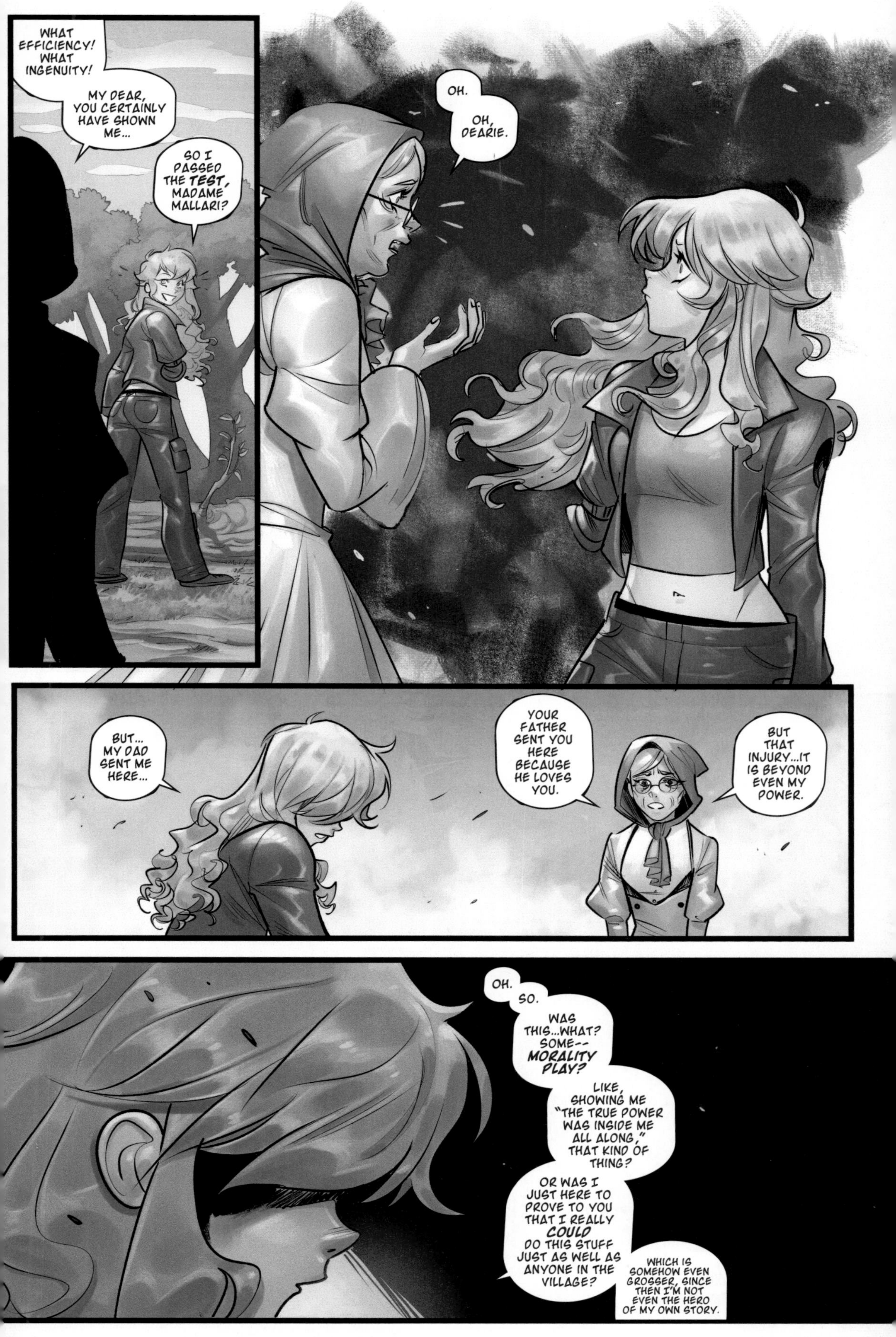
WHAT EFFICIENCY! WHAT INGENUITY!
MY DEAR, YOU CERTAINLY HAVE SHOWN ME...
SO I PASSED THE TEST, MADAME MALLARI?
OH.
OH, DEARIE.
BUT... MY DAD SENT ME HERE...
YOUR FATHER SENT YOU HERE BECAUSE HE LOVES YOU.
BUT THAT INJURY...IT IS BEYOND EVEN MY POWER.
OH.
SO.
WAS THIS...WHAT? SOME-- MORALITY PLAY?
LIKE, SHOWING ME "THE TRUE POWER WAS INSIDE ME ALL ALONG," THAT KIND OF THING?
OR WAS I JUST HERE TO PROVE TO YOU THAT I REALLY COULD DO THIS STUFF JUST AS WELL AS ANYONE IN THE VILLAGE?
WHICH IS SOMEHOW EVEN GROSSER, SINCE THEN I'M NOT EVEN THE HERO OF MY OWN STORY.

OH, DEARIE, YANG!
I SWEAR, YOU THINK MORE THAN ANYONE ELSE GIVES YOU CREDIT FOR.
AT BEACON ACADEMY, DID ANY OF YOUR PROFESSORS REALIZE YOU WERE MORE THAN AN ANIMATE CLOUD OF YELLOW HAIR SHOUTING ABOUT YOUR BABY SISTER AND BRANDISHING MORE WEAPONS THAN ONE?
THE WORLD, AND THE LIFE WITHIN IT, IS NOT AND HAS NEVER BEEN FAIR.
AND THOUGH IT HAS NEVER BEEN FAIR, YOU ARE AND WILL ALWAYS HAVE TO BE YOUR OWN BEST HEALER.
"THERE ARE THOSE WHO CAN SHORTEN THE JOURNEY.
"THOSE WHO WILL HELP CARRY ITS BURDENS.
"THOSE WHO WILL SHARE THEIR TIME AND WARMTH AND LIGHT WITH YOU.
"BUT IN THE END, IT WILL ALWAYS BE YOURS.
"WHETHER YOU HATE IT, REJOICE IN IT, RESENT IT, LEARN WHAT YOU CAN FROM IT, IGNORE IT, BEAR IT, STRUGGLE WITH IT, SUFFER FROM IT--
"--IT IS YOURS, AND NO ONE ELSE'S."

JUST AS I HAD TO IN MY YOUTH.
OR DID YOU THINK YOUR FATHER ONLY OFFERED YOUR AID BECAUSE I AM OLD.
HOW--?
NONE OF YOUR BUSINESS.
JUST AS NONE OF WHAT YOU DO OR FEEL OR THINK IS ANYONE ELSE'S BUSINESS.
UNTIL YOU DECIDE TO SHARE IT WITH THEM.
YOUR BODY IS YOUR OWN, INVIOLATE.
IT WILL CHANGE AND ALTER, HURT AND HEAL, AND THE WORLD WILL TREAT YOU DIFFERENTLY, AND YOU MUST LEARN TO TREAT YOURSELF IN NEW WAYS, TOO.
A BODY IS NOT YOUR BEING, BUT IT IS A TOOL--
SOMETHING THAT CAN BE USED FOR GOOD OR FOR EVIL, BUT ONLY AT YOUR OWN WILL.
YOUR SPIRIT, YOUR CHOICES, YOUR REASONS--THESE DEFINE YOUR BODY, NOT THE WORLD, AND NOT WHAT HAS BEEN DONE TO YOU.
YOUR COURAGE AND FEARLESSNESS ARE UNCHANGED, BUT YOU MUST LEARN TO OFFER THAT KINDNESS AND PATIENCE TO YOURSELF AS WELL.
THANK YOU FOR TODAY, YANG XIAO LONG.
THANK YOU FOR TODAY, MADAME MALLARI.

I'M HOME!
OOOF, IS THAT THE RIPE, TANGY SMELL OF VICTORY?
HIIII, DAD.
OKAY, LET'S TRY THIS AGAIN...
The Man With Two Souls
"HIS FRIENDS WERE THOSE OF HIS OWN BLOOD OR THOSE WHOM HE HAD KNOWN THE LONGEST...
The Man With Two Souls
"HIS AFFECTIONS, LIKE IVY, WERE THE GROWTH OF TIME."

THE SEA OF MENAGERIE. NOW.
I RAN.
AGAIN.
RUBY, WEISS...
YANG...
SUNFLOWER POP
AFTER THE BATTLE OF BEACON, I RAN OUT--ON ALL OF THEM.
IT WAS THE ONLY WAY TO SAVE THEM.
TO SAVE ANYONE I GET TOO CLOSE TO.
SO MANY TIMES, I SHOULD HAVE BEEN AFRAID WHEN I WASN'T.
MENAGERIE. YEARS AGO.
IF ONLY I HAD RUN BACK THEN...
...THE NIGHT I SAW THE REAL ADAM TAURUS.
I AM SIENNA KHAN, A LOYAL ADVOCATE FOR THE WHITE FANG, WHICH FIGHTS FOR THE LIBERATION OF ALL FAUNUS!
Blake: Part I
Intoxication
Marguerite Bennett Writer
Mirka Andolfo Artist
Arif Prianto Colorist
Gabriela Downie Letterer
Andrew Marino Editor

I BRING GRAVE NEWS FROM OUR OPERATIVES ADAM TAURUS AND ILIA AMITOLA--
TODAY THREE MEMBERS OF THE WHITE FANG WERE CAPTURED BY VICIOUS HUMAN MERCENARIES, ALL FOR TRYING TO HELP FAUNUS WHO WERE ABUSED AND MISTREATED IN THE DUST MINES!
WE FEAR FOR THE LIVES OF OUR IMPRISONED BROTHERS AND SISTER, AS WE CAN ONLY IMAGINE THE HORRORS INFLICTED ON THE CAPTIVE FAUNUS--
MOM, I DON'T... FEEL SO GOOD. CAN I GO BACK HOME?
BLAKE--?
PLEASE, IT'S JUST A FEW BLOCKS--
THE WHITE FANG WISHES TO ACKNOWLEDGE GHIRA AND KALI BELLADONNA FOR THEIR PEACEKEEPING EFFORTS AMID THIS CHAOS--

THE WHITE FANG REMAINS COMMITTED TO THE LIBERATION OF THE FAUNUS, AND THESE RADICALS WITHIN OUR RANKS MUST NOT BE PERMITTED TO CORRUPT OUR MESSAGE--
?!
SOB
SNRRL
SOB
H-HELLO--?
I SHOULD'VE BEEN FRIGHTENED...
...BUT I WASN'T.
YOU--
YOU SAW--
I WAS...
...SPELLBOUND.

YOU CAN'T--
DON'T YOU DARE TELL ANYONE!
I WON'T.
I DIDN'T FLINCH.
I DIDN'T RUN.
I KNEW WHAT WAS BEHIND THE MASK.
DID A SINGLE OTHER SOUL KNOW?
THE THREE FAUNUS WHO WERE CAPTURED IN VALE...
...THEY WERE YOUR FRIENDS, WEREN'T THEY?
I'M SORRY.
...
YOU'RE GHIRA BELLADONNA'S DAUGHTER. OUT ALONE IN THE STREETS AT NIGHT.
OUR HOUSE IS CLOSE.
STILL. SO LATE AT NIGHT.
"LET ME--LET ME WALK WITH YOU.
"YOU NEVER KNOW WHAT MONSTERS ARE OUT IN THE DARK."
HE DIDN'T KISS MY HAND. DIDN'T THREATEN. DIDN'T JOKE.
IT WOULD BE A YEAR BEFORE I SAW HIM IN DAYLIGHT.

ONE YEAR LATER.
A SECRET GATHERING OF THE WHITE FANG.
BLAKE...
...I THINK YOU KNOW ADAM TAURUS.
KNOW HIM?
OF COURSE I KNEW HIM.
YOU CAME BACK.
AFTER YOUR FATHER WITHDREW HIS SUPPORT FOR ALL US "RADICALS" IN THE WHITE FANG.
YOU'RE STILL HERE.
THE SAME COULD BE SAID OF YOU.
YOU COULD GET OUT--TURN YOURSELF IN. DO PENANCE.
ASK FOR PARDON FOR THE EXTREME MEASURES YOU'VE TAKEN.
YOU'D HAVE A NEW LIFE.
AND YOU KNOW WHY I CAN'T.
I WANT A BETTER WORLD FOR THE FAUNUS.
MY FAMILY IS SECURE, BUT SO MANY OTHERS...
YOU'RE NOT AFRAID.
NOTHING YOU COULD DO WOULD FRIGHTEN ME.

DUST MINE #435.
WE FOUGHT TOGETHER, MISSION AFTER MISSION.
RESCUED FAUNUS BEHIND ENEMY LINES, FREED PRISONERS FROM SCHNEE DUST COMPANY MERCENARIES.
EIGHTEEN MONTHS BEFORE YOU LEAVE HIM.
IT WAS LIKE BEING IN A WHIRLWIND, A RIPTIDE
I'M NOT AFRAID OF THIS.
WE SHOULD HAVE RUN AWAY AND LEFT IT ALL BEHIND.
THE HARBOR OF HAVEN.
SIX MONTHS BEFORE YOU LEAVE HIM.

...I WAS INTOXICATED.
NO.
DON'T TOUCH IT.
I'M NOT AFRAID OF YOU.
THOUGH I SHOULD HAVE BEEN.
AIRSPACE OVER MENAGERIE.
A YEAR BEFORE YOU LEAVE HIM.
ADAM...
...I'M NOT AFRAID.

THE BELLADONNA HOUSE.
THE NIGHT BEFORE YOU LEAVE HIM.
THE BOILER ROOM.
--HEARD THE LATEST NEWS ABOUT THESE RADICALS WHO HAVE TAKEN OVER THE WHITE FANG--
--LIKE RABID DOGS--
BLAKE--?
ADAM.
I HEARD ABOUT YOUR LATEST "MISSION." SIX DEAD-- SIX!
IT WAS TEN.
I DON'T...
HOW CAN THIS BE?
THE BOY WHO I FOUND CRYING IN AN ALLEY OVER THE CAPTURE OF HIS FRIENDS--
HOW CAN THAT BE THE MAN STANDING IN FRONT OF ME?!
I WASN'T CRYING FOR THEM.
MY ONLY REGRET, BLAKE, WAS FOR THE HUMANS.
AND THAT OUR FALLEN WHITE FANG BROTHERS--
--COULD NOT HAVE KILLED A HUNDRED THOUSAND MORE.

THAT.
YOU DON'T KNOW WHAT I AM.
YOUR LOVE IS GOING TO SAVE ME?
EVER GOING TO LET IT?
OR DID YOU THINK *THIS* MADE YOU A MONSTER?
OH, ADAM...
IT WAS NEVER YOUR FACE.
TOMORROW.
THE TRAIN HEIST.
ARE YOU AFRAID?
I PROMISED YOU, ADAM...
...I'LL NEVER BE AFRAID

THE SEA OF MENAGERIE.
INTOXICATION... JUST A FANCY WORD FOR ITS OWN HEART.
TOXIC.
IS THAT WHAT I AM?
POISON?
DO I POISON EVERYONE AROUND ME?
DO I THINK I CAN SAVE PEOPLE, ONLY TO LIVE TO SEE HOW MUCH WORSE THEY BECOME FOR EVER KNOWING ME?!
YOU CAN'T DO THAT AGAIN, BLAKE.
CAN'T EVER GET CLOSE TO ANYONE, EVER AGAIN.
RUBY AND WEISS AND...Y-YANG...
THIS IS THE ONLY WAY TO SAVE THEM.
SUNFLOWER POP
I WISH I'D BEEN AFRAID.
SUNFLOWER POP
NEXT:
THE WOE'S OF WEISS SCHNEE

THE SCHNEE MANOR. NOW.
WEISS, SWEETHEART, PLEASE, DON'T SULK!
YOU ARE NOT THE FIRST SCHNEE IN HISTORY TO SUFFER DISAPPOINTMENT, AND THIS BEHAVIOR IS REALLY RATHER EXCESSIVE...
IT IS NATURAL TO BE UNHAPPY TO LEAVE BEACON ACADEMY, BUT FRIENDS COME AND GO, AND GO MORE OFTEN AS THEY GET OLDER...
...BUT FAMILY IS FOREVER.
MY PARENTS HAD ME FETCHED FROM BEACON THE DAY AFTER THE ATTACK.
OUR FAMILY HAS ALWAYS BEEN INFLUENTIAL. WEALTHY. FAMOUS, REALLY.
OUR NAME GOES BACK A HUNDRED YEARS, AND MY FATHER MADE THE SCHNEE DUST COMPANY INTO... A TITAN.
MY SISTER, WINTER, IS THE PERFECT HEIR TO THE FAMILY THRONE.
BUT I WAS...WELL.
WHAT'S THAT PHRASE ABOUT THE DUTY OF A QUEEN? THE ONE ABOUT PROVIDING TWO CHILDREN?
"AN HEIR, AND A SPARE."
THEY WANTED ME KEPT WAITING IN THE WINGS, READY WHEN NEEDED.
PURE AND PERFECT AND SHELTERED...
A SNOWFLAKE IN A SNOW GLOBE.
Weiss Part I:
Look at Me
Marguerite Bennett Writer
Mirka Andolfo Pencils
Gabriele Bagnoli Inks
Arif Prianto Colors
Gabriela Downie Letters
Sarah Stone Cover
Stanley "Artgerm" Lau Variant Cover
Andrew Marino Editor
UNTIL A YEAR AGO, WHEN I MADE MY CHOICE, DISOBEYED, AND JOINED BEACON ACADEMY TO BECOME A HUNTRESS...
...I BROKE THE GLASS...

...AND BECAME A SNOWFLAKE IN A STORM.
BEACON ACADEMY. THEN.
I WAS--SECURE IN MY FAMILY'S STANDING WHEN I FIRST ARRIVED AT BEACON.
BUT I KNOW BETTER WORDS NOW FOR WHAT I WAS THEN...HAUGHTY. VAIN. RUDE.
I'D LIVED MY ENTIRE LIFE IN THAT LITTLE GLASS BUBBLE.
AND THERE IS A GREAT DIFFERENCE BETWEEN "BREAKING OUT" AND "BREAKING IN."
MY INTRODUCTION TO THE WORST THE WORLD HAD TO OFFER WAS CALLED--
Volume
LOOK AT ME.
PROFESSOR GOODWITCH'S CLASS.
MS. SCHNEE, WHAT COMMAND OF THE CRAFT!
PROFESSOR PORT'S CLASS.
LOOK AT ME.
100
AN EXCELLENT SCORE AGAIN, MS. SCHNEE!

--CARDIN WINCHESTER.
ICE PRINCESS IS JUST HERE BECAUSE HER DAD DONATED, LIKE, A WHOLE WING TO THE SCHOOL.
I BET THEY EVEN NAME IT "THE SCHNEE INSTITUTE FOR WHICH SILVER SOUP SPOON TO USE."
DID YOU KNOW SCHNEE ISN'T EVEN HER DAD'S NAME? IT'S HER MOM'S! HE TOOK IT WHEN THEY GOT MARRIED!
CARDIN, THAT IS UNKIND.
AND WHO TAKES WHOSE NAME IS HARDLY ANY BUSINESS OF YOURS--
YOU DON'T KNOW ANYTHING ABOUT WEISS SCHNEE!
SHOOT, PYRRHA'S JUST AS BAD. SO HOLIER-THAN-THOU.
JUST WAIT UNTIL TRAINING DAY. I'LL SEE TO IT ALL OF THOSE STUCK-UP, KNOW-IT-ALL BATTLE-AXES GET WHAT'S COMING TO THEM--
THEY THOUGHT I WAS ONLY THERE BECAUSE OF MY NAME. MY FATHER. OUR COMPANY. OUR MONEY.
YOU'RE GOING TO LEARN HOW WRONG YOU ARE, CARDIN WINCHESTER.
I'LL PROVE I BELONG HERE.
JUST WATCH.
AFTER PROFESSOR OOBLECK'S CLASS.
LOOK AT ME NOW.
HEY, DON'T CRY--IT WAS ONE BAD LESSON!
LOOK, NO ONE IS BORN KNOWING THIS STUFF.
DO YOU WANT TO MAYBE... PRACTICE TOGETHER?
IF CARDIN WINCHESTER WAS MY INTRODUCTION TO THE WORST MY NEW WORLD HAD TO OFFER, THEN THE BEST BY FAR...
...WAS TEAM RWBY.

THE COURTYARD. SPRING.
STUDENTS! TODAY YOUR PROFESSORS HAVE PREPARED AN OBSTACLE COURSE TO TEST YOUR ABILITIES AS THEY NOW STAND.
PERHAPS ITS KNOWLEDGE, THOUGH UNTRANSLATED IN OUR AGE, WILL BRING WISDOM TO A NEW GENERATION.
THE WINNER WILL RECEIVE A RARE ARTIFACT FROM OUR LIBRARY!
THE OBSTACLE COURSE LIES AHEAD. THE FIRST TO OUTWIT ITS DANGERS AND CROSS THE FINISH LINE, BY WHATEVER MEANS NECESSARY, IS OUR VICTOR!
DID HE REALLY JUST SAY "BY WHATEVER MEANS NECESSARY?"
FREE-FOR-ALLS TEST US AGAINST OPPONENTS SMARTER THAN GRIMM, BABY SISTER.
YANG'S THE STRONGEST. PERHAPS WE SHOULD FOCUS ON GETTING HER ACROSS THE FINISH LINE--
I JUST WANT SOMEONE FROM TEAM RWBY TO WIN.
SO LONG AS IT'S NOT--
TCH. NOT A SINGLE OPPONENT WORTHY OF ME.
TOO BAD PYRRHA ISN'T COMPETING--MUST NOT WANT TO GET THOSE BOOTS DIRTY AFTER JAUNE LICKED THEM CLEAN.
DID YOU KNOW HE'S SO AWFUL AT COMBAT, HE TAKES EXTRA LESSONS WITH HER? PATHETIC!
REMEMBER--THIS IS A FREE-FOR-ALL!
ON YOUR MARK!
GET SET!

BOOOOOM
WEISS, I JUST...DON'T UNDERSTAND WHY YOU'RE BEHAVING THIS WAY.
AGILITY, STUDENTS!
YANG!
OOF
COMBAT!
WHAT DO YOU THINK OF THIS, CARDIN?
YOU ACT AS THOUGH YOU'VE BEEN KIDNAPPED OR IMPRISONED--
--AND THAT SIMPLY IS NOT WHAT HAPPENED.
AAAH!
?!
MY WEAPON!

AND IF YOU DID HAVE TO LEAVE THOSE RADICALS, THOSE... "FRIENDS" BEHIND, WELL... ALL THE BETTER.
NEXT UP, STUDENTS--
--LOGIC!
SOLVE YOUR GLYPH-LOCK TO PROCEED AHEAD!
"WEISS, I LOVE YOU, BUT YOU ARE REALLY QUITE OVERREACTING TO THE WHOLE THING."
I DON'T HAVE TIME FOR THIS--
CRNCH
NOT SO SLICK NOW, ICE PRINCESS--
"AT A CERTAIN POINT, YOU HAVE TO TAKE RESPONSIBILITY FOR YOUR ROLE IN ALL OF THIS."
SPRINT, STUDENTS!
IT'S THE FINAL STRETCH!

COME ON, CARDIN, WEREN'T YOU SCARED YOU WEREN'T GOING TO HAVE A WORTHY OPPONENT?
STOP-- DODGING--
WHY? I'M PRETTY SURE YOU'RE THE ICE PRINCE, CARDIN, NOT ME.
YOU STUCK-UP--
JUST LOOK AT THAT...
...YOU'RE EVEN MELTING.
WHY DON'T YOU COOL OFF?
"AND YOU'LL ONLY HAVE YOURSELF TO ANSWER TO."
IF YOU CHOOSE TO CONTINUE IN THIS WAY, WEISS...
...THEN WE WILL HAVE NO CHOICE BUT TO KEEP YOU HERE.
STUDENTS AND TEACHERS, CLASSMATES AND PRO-FESSORS...
...WE HAVE OUR VICTOR!

BEACON ACADEMY, MAY WE PRESENT THE VICTOR OF TODAY'S COMPETITION--
WEISS! WEISS! WEISS! WEISS!
WOOOOOOO
STOP!
SHE--SHE CHEATED!
I DON'T KNOW HOW--
--BUT THERE'S NO WAY SOME ENTITLED, RICH LITTLE BRAT WHOSE DADDY PAID FOR HER TO GET IN COULD--EVER--BEAT--SOMEONE--LIKE ME!
ELUSIONAL...
EVERYONE SAW!
JERK.
WHAT A BABY!
SORE LOSER.
THE ONLY ENTITLEMENT I SEE, CARDIN, IS YOUR REFUSAL TO ACCEPT THAT YOU WERE BEATEN.
YEEAAH, WEEIIISS!
WHOO! WHOO! WHOO! WHOO!

IN THE FOREST, I SAW THE STUNT YOU PULLED WITH THE DUST, WEISS.
WHAT STUNT?
YOU TRICKED CARDIN. MADE HIM THINK THERE WAS A BEOWOLF WHEN IT WAS ONLY GLYPHS IN THE AIR. THEN TRICKED HIM INTO OVER-EXTENDING HIMSELF.
AND YOU MUST'VE KNOWN HOW HE'D REACT TO LOSING.
WELL, IT WASN'T CHEATING.
IT WASN'T THE POINT OF THE EXERCISE EITHER.
IT'S NOT MY FAULT IF HE HASN'T GOT TWO BRAIN CELLS TO RUB TOGETHER FOR FLINT AND TINDER!
BUT YOU ARE THE ONE WHO GUARANTEED HE'D BE SEEN AS A CRAZY LAUGHING-STOCK IN FRONT OF ALL OUR CLASS-MATES.
SNAP
I DIDN'T MEAN FOR HIM TO GET HUMILIATED IN FRONT OF THE ENTIRE SCHOOL. IF HE'D ONLY ACCEPTED HE ISN'T AS AMAZING AS HE BRAGS TO EVERYONE--
SO HE DESERVED IT, RIGHT?
BLAKE, WHY ARE YOU UPSET?
I'M NOT UPSET.
AFTER ALL HE'S DONE TO JAUNE, TO PYRRHA, TO--
WEISS. YOU AND CARDIN HAVE BEEN IN EACH OTHER'S CROSSHAIRS SINCE WELL BEFORE CARDIN TARGETED EITHER OF THEM.
I THINK AS LITTLE OF CARDIN AND HIS BEHAVIOR AS RUBY, YANG, NORA, REN--AS ANYONE DOES.
BUT I THINK QUITE A BIT MORE OF YOU.
AND I REALLY THINK YOU SHOULD EXAMINE HOW COMFORTABLE YOU ARE WITH THE TACTICS YOU USED TODAY.
I HOPE THAT BOOK WAS WORTH IT.

I KNOW I'VE BEEN GIVEN A LOT. I'VE HAD SO MUCH JUST HANDED TO ME BY MY FAMILY, BUT THIS ONE THING...MY LIFE AS A HUNTRESS...
...IT'S SOMETHING I HAD TO EARN MYSELF.
AND I HAVE!
WEISS, THAT WAS INCREDIBLE!
WHEN PEOPLE SEE ME NOW, THEY DON'T SEE MY FATHER, HIS COMPANY, OUR MONEY, OUR NAME...
YOU DODGED THOSE THINGS LIKE IT WAS NOTHING!
AND THE LOGIC PUZZLE--
...THEY THINK OF MY DETERMINATION TO BE THE BEST OF US ALL.
AND LOOK AT ME, BLAKE, LOOK AT ME..
SCHNEE MANOR.
...LOOK AT ME NOW.
WEISS? SWEET-HEART? ARE YOU LISTENING TO ME?

The Forest of Hinoki.
The Continent of Anima.
FLUTT'R
FLUTTER
FLUTT'R
RUBY, WHAT'S WRONG?
I JUST WATCHED THESE BABY BIRDS FLY AWAY, BUT LOOK...
...THIS ONE DIDN'T HATCH. IT'S COLD AS A STONE.
THAT'S HARD.
THE BIRDS HAVE TO WORK TO BREAK THE SHELLS THEMSELVES. IT'S THE ONLY WAY THEY'LL BE STRONG ENOUGH TO FLY WHEN THE TIME COMES.
YOU COULDN'T HAVE HELPED IT.
IT HAD TO DO THE WORK ITSELF.
RUBY!
A GRIMM IS ATTACKING!
COME ON! WE CAN HELP!
THIS IS WHAT HUNTSMEN ARE MADE FOR!

Ruby: Part 2
The Egg
Marguerite Bennett Writer
Meghan Hetrick Artist
Arif Prianto Colorist
Gabriela Downie Letterer
Andrew Marino Editor
GET BACK, YOU VILE HUNTSMEN!
HUNTSMEN?!
LOOK OUT!
THEY'RE FROM BEACON!
HWWW--
--ARRRRG!
ALL RIGHT, TEAM RNJR! WE CAN DO THIS, RIGHT?
BEST GRIMM-GRINDING HUNTSMEN FROM BEACON ACADEMY, AND--
RUBY! NOT THAT FORMATION!
WHA--

NOT ON TEAM RWBY ANYMORE. TEAM RNJR NOW, TEAM RNJR--
--AHH!
FWOOSH
NOT YANG, NOT BLAKE, NOT WEISS--
GRRRRRR--
--IT'S NORA, REN, JAUNE, AND--
NOW, RUBY!
--ME!

OW, OW, OW--
RUBY, ARE YOU HURT?!
NO, NO! IT'S FINE! JUST-- MUSCLES I-- HAVEN'T HAD-- TO STRETCH IN A WHILE.
DIFFERENT FIGHTING STYLE. SOMETIMES, WHEN TEAM JNPR HAS TO TAKE ON A BIG BAD, WE HAVE TO STAND OUR GROUND.
PYRRHA TAUGHT US THAT.
IF ONE OF US BREAKS THE LINE, ALL OF US WILL GET BROKEN, AND THEN--
TUNK
YOWCH!
GET AWAY FROM HERE, YOU VILLAINS!
YOU'RE THE ONES WHO NEED TO GET AWAY!
MANTICORES RARELY TRAVEL ALONE. IF THIS ONE WANDERED OFF, THERE ARE LIKELY TEN MORE OUT THERE THAT COULD BE HEADING THIS WAY!
AS THOUGH I WOULD TRUST FILTHY HUNTSMEN--
WHAT IS YOUR PROBLEM WITH HUNTSMEN, HUH?!

ALL OF REMNANT HEARD THE MESSAGE BROADCAST FROM BEACON, JUST BEFORE THE ACADEMY FELL!
THAT BLACK QUEEN SPEAKING TO US...
...REVEALING THE TRUTH OF WHAT THOSE SCHOOLS HAVE BEEN TRAINING...HAVE BEEN MAKING!
YOU HUNTSMEN ARE NO MORE THAN PRIVATE ARMIES, BENT ON OPEN WAR!
WE ALL SAW THE BEACON STUDENT OBLITERATE THAT--AUTOMATON FROM ATLAS! THAT MACHINE MASQUERADING AS AN INNOCENT GIRL!
ROBOTS AND RENEGADES, CHILD SOLDIERS AND SECRET POLICE--
--BEACON HUNTSMEN ARE INVADERS IN ANIMA, THAT'S WHAT YOU ALL ARE!
YOU PRETEND TO COME HERE TO SLAY THE GRIMM, BUT YOU ONLY PLAN TO LURE US INTO LETTING DOWN OUR DEFENSES. THEN YOU'LL SLAUGHTER US FROM INSIDE!
WE HAVE SEALED THE VILLAGE EVER SINCE! TURNED AWAY OUR NEIGHBORS, LEST THEY'RE YOUR SPIES!
WE'RE WISE TO YOUR ACT, YOU--YOU MARAUDERS, YOU THUGS--

"--MARAUDERS OF BEACON!"
THIS IS AWFUL.
IF WE DON'T HELP THEM, THEN THE REST OF THE MANTICORES COME FOR THEM, THEY GET KILLED, AND--I CANNOT STRESS ENOUGH THAT THIS IS SECONDARY--WE'LL GET BLAMED FOR NOT HELPING THEM.
IF WE DO HELP THEM, THEY DON'T GET KILLED, AND THEY STILL BLAME US FOR TRYING TO STEAL THEIR VILLAGE OR WHATEVER--
--ALL BECAUSE THEY LISTENED TO CINDER'S HORRIBLE BROADCAST!
WHY... ARE THEY SO SCARED OF US?
YEAH, WE'RE FROM BEACON, BUT IT'S FOUR OF US AGAINST HOW MANY OF THEM?
AND THEY'RE ADULTS! THEY'RE SUPPOSED TO KNOW BETTER!
WELL...

...OVER THE YEARS THAT THE GREAT WAR WAS FOUGHT, HUMANITY DEVELOPED MORE EFFICIENT AND POWERFUL WAYS TO DESTROY ONE ANOTHER.
WHEN THE WAR WAS OVER, THE WORLD CHOSE TO TAKE ALL OF THEIR NEWFOUND LESSONS IN VIOLENCE...
...AND TEACH THEM TO *THEIR CHILDREN.*
NOW, WE HUNT *GRIMM*--WE'RE *NOT* SOLDIERS, WE'RE *NOT* AN ARMY, AND WE DON'T HURT *PEOPLE.*
BUT IT'S HARD NOT TO REMEMBER THE OLD WAR AND THE OLD WAYS, AND WONDER...
...IF THE WARS COME AGAIN, WILL THESE CHILDREN BECOME SOLDIERS?
AND IF THEY DO, *WHAT POWER IN THE WORLD COULD STOP THEM?*

HWAAAARG!
THE GRIMM...
...THEY'VE COME BACK.
I DON'T CARE IF THESE VILLAGERS THINK WE'RE BAD OR GOOD.
PENNY WAS GOOD. PYRRHA WAS GOOD.
IT'S HARD TO GRIEVE, HARD TO FORGIVE, HARD TO CHANGE, HARD TO GROW...
!
...HARD TO LEAVE BEHIND, HARD TO MOVE AHEAD, HARD TO DO ANYTHING WORTH ANYTHING.
THAT'S THE ONLY WAY TO BEAT THE GRIMM, AND CINDER, AND EVERYTHING BAD IN THE WORLD.
EVEN WHEN IT'S HARD--

THESE MEAN, SCARED, IGNORANT PEOPLE--MAYBE THEY DON'T DESERVE GOOD.
BUT THEY STILL DESERVE TO LIVE.
IT'S HARD TO HEAL.
IT'S HARD TO LEARN.
I JUST--WHAT IN LIFE ISN'T HARD?
BUT YOU JUST NEED TO KEEP LIVING.
--JUST LIVE.
...

I DON'T WANT A THANK-YOU. I WOULDN'T SAY "YOU'RE WELCOME."
YOU WANT TO LISTEN TO SCARE TACTICS INSTEAD OF THINKING FOR YOURSELF, THAT'S YOUR CHOICE.
YOU WANT TO BELIEVE WHAT SOME STRANGER TELLS YOU INSTEAD OF WHAT YOUR EYES AND EARS SHOW YOU, THAT'S YOUR CHOICE.
BUT BIRDS THAT DON'T HATCH JUST DIE IN THEIR EGGS.
SO I HOPE YOU CHOOSE TO BREAK OUT. OPEN UP. TRUST PEOPLE AND HELP PEOPLE. GROW.
EVEN IF IT'S HARD.
BUT I CAN'T MAKE YOU DO IT.
AND I CAN'T DO IT FOR YOU.
WE KEPT WALKING.
THROUGH THE STORM, WE HEARD THEM CALL TO US.
THEY CALLED US BACK.
THERE WAS NOTHING THERE FOR US. NOTHING WE NEEDED. NOTHING MORE WE COULD OFFER.
WE HAD DONE WHAT WE COULD FOR THEM.
BECAUSE FINALLY, WE HEARD THE SOUNDS OF GEARS AND METAL.
FINALLY...
...THEY'D OPENED THE GATES.
NEXT:
Yang and Blake's Night to Remember

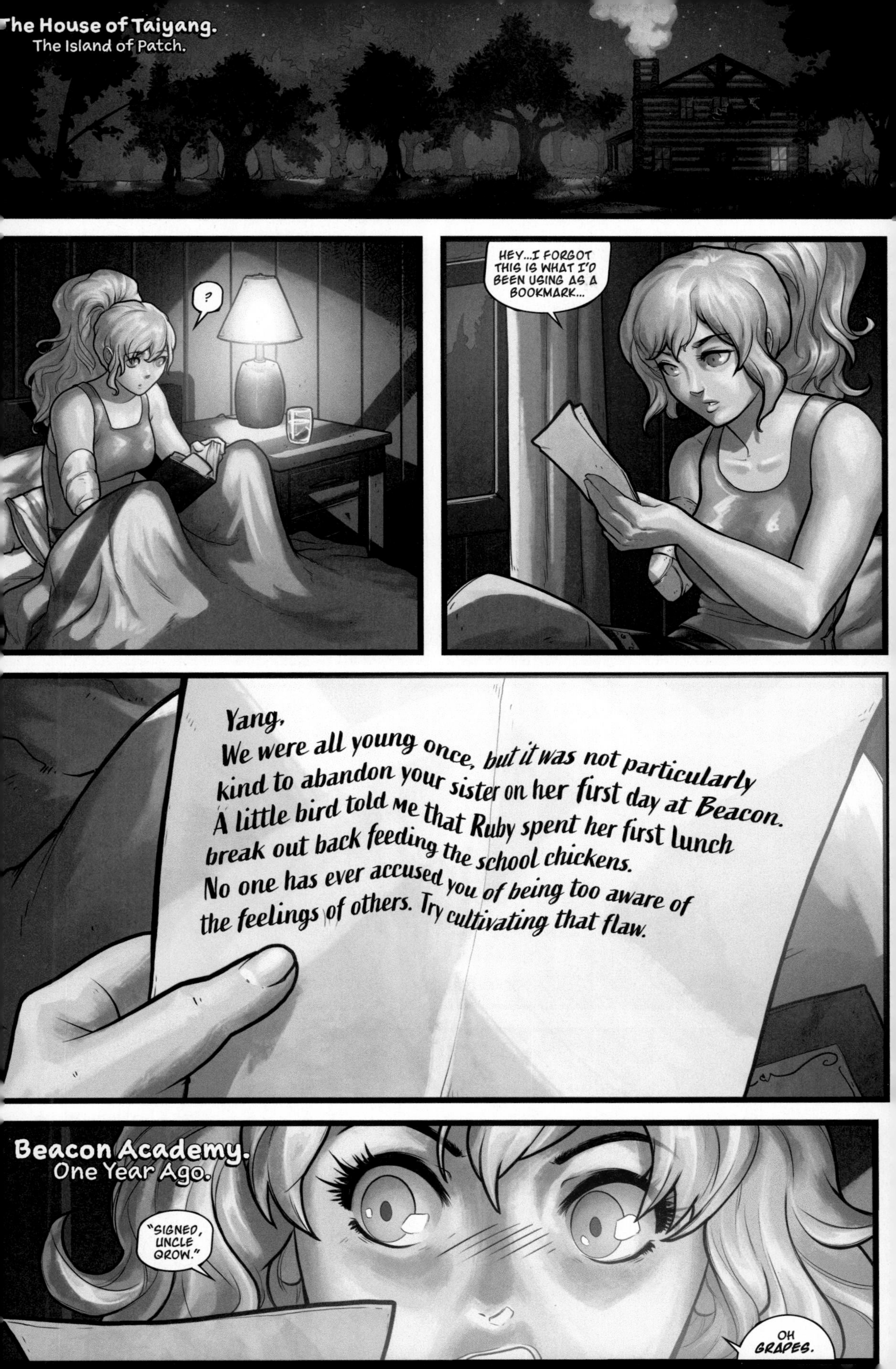

The House of Taiyang.
The Island of Patch.
?
HEY...I FORGOT THIS IS WHAT I'D BEEN USING AS A BOOKMARK...
Yang,
We were all young once, but it was not particularly kind to abandon your sister on her first day at Beacon. A little bird told me that Ruby spent her first lunch break out back feeding the school chickens. No one has ever accused you of being too aware of the feelings of others. Try cultivating that flaw.
Beacon Academy.
One Year Ago.
"SIGNED, UNCLE QROW."
OH GRAPES.

RUBY! BABY SISTER!
I SCREWED UP SO BAD! CHICKENS! YOU HAD TO EAT LUNCH WITH CHICKENS!
YANG-- --MY LUNGS-- --MY ADORABLE BUT EXTREMELY CRUSHABLE LUNGS!
WHEEZE
DON'T WORRY ABOUT IT, YANG!
WHEEZE
I GOT TO FEED THE CHICKENS!
WHEEZE
CHICKENS ARE GREAT!
I'LL BE A BETTER SISTER AND A BETTER FRIEND! I'M STARTING TODAY, I PROMISE!
THOSE ARE MAGIC WORDS, RIGHT?
SURE, IN THE "THERE'S ACTUALLY NO SUCH THING AS MAGIC" SENSE!
HEY, WEISS, YOU NEED EXTRA HELP WITH YOUR HOMEWORK?
HAVE I EVER?
HEY, HAVE YOU MET MY SISTER, RUBY?
...DO I KNOW YOU?
HEY, YANG, YOU'RE RIGHT! THIS DOES MAKE ME FEEL A LITTLE LESS HOMESICK!
FULL BIG-SISTER TREATMENT, BOOM.
HOW ABOUT YOU, UH...

...BLAKE?
The Rodeo.
"HELP YOU COME OUT OF YOUR SHELL?
The Lake.
"DISCOVER NEW HOBBIES?
The Dinner Party.
"EAT A BALANCED DIET?"
OU DON'T NEED TO HELP ME, YANG--
MAY I HELP YOU, PLEASE?
MAGIC WORDS, RIGHT?!
WHY DON'T YOU TRY THIS? IT'S ABOUT A MAN WITH TWO SOULS.
HE MIGHT HAVE ENOUGH ENERGY TO KEEP UP WITH ALL YOUR ACTIVITIES.
...AND OF COURSE IT'S SO DRY AND DUSTY, I CAN'T GET PAST THE FIRST CHAPTER.
YOU KNOW WHAT, THAT'S WHAT SHE NEEDS! THE OPPOSITE OF DRY AND DUSTY--

--COPIOUS AMOUNTS OF HEAVILY CAFFEINATED LIQUID COURAGE.
DRANKY'S
TONITE
THIS PLACE IS GREAT!
THUMPIN' BANDS, STRONG DRINKS, REAL AUTHENTIC, EXCITING, ADRENALINE-FILLED FUN!
THE HARPEES
TWO SUNFLOWER POPS, PLEASE!
HEY, CHECK THIS OUT--
POP
FSSSSSSS
SUNFLOWER POP!
TO YOUR HEALTH.
TEN POINTS!
SHUT THE DOOR!
SHUT ME
CLOSE
OOOH, THE BAND'S STARTING UP!

I STARTED READING THE BOOK YOU LENT ME! IT'S SO DARK!
HEY, IF YOU THINK THAT'S SPOOKY, YOU SHOULD TRY THE CORPSE DOCTOR OR THE VAMPIRE COUNT--
DO YOU JUST LIKE HORROR BOOKS?
I LIKE ALL KINDS OF BOOKS, BUT SCARY STORIES LIKE THAT--THEY MAKE MY HEART RACE, THRILL ME, EXHILARATE ME--BUT I ALWAYS KNOW I'M STILL SAFE.
WOW.
AND YOU LEARN SO MUCH BY READING THEM--THE CORPSE DOCTOR IS REALLY ABOUT THE HORROR AND RESPONSIBILITY OF CREATION.
THE UNDEAD IS ULTIMATELY ABOUT YOUR FEAR OF OTHER PEOPLE.
THE VAMPIRE COUNT IS THE FEAR OF THE OTHER, CONTAMINATION, AND THE LOSS OF CONTROL OVER WOMEN--
YOU ARE...SO SMART, YOU KNOW THAT? I COULD LISTEN TO YOU ALL DAY.
HEH. WELL, IT'S FUN TO ANALYZE--YOU MIGHT LIKE IT, TOO.
SCARY STORIES, THEY ALL REPRESENT DIFFERENT THINGS.
AND THE MAN WITH TWO SOULS?
REPRESENTS SOMETHING YOU DIDN'T KNOW YOU HAD INSIDE YOU.
BUT UNLIKE THE BOOK, IT ISN'T ALWAYS BAD.
SOMETIMES...
...IT'S EXCITING.
SUNFLOWER POP!
SUNFLOWER POP!
CLNK

REALLY EXCITING.
THIS THE BUTTERCUP WHO ROUGHED UP YOUR BROTHERS?
JUNIOR TOLD ME WE WERE SQUARE.
SNORT
JUNIOR'S THEIR EMPLOYER.
"I'M THEIR MOM."
BASH!!

A Few Broken Bottles, Bones, and Bears Later.
INSANE! THAT FIGHT WAS INSANE!
HOW IS THAT SALOON STILL STANDING--?
FWOOOOOM
HRMPH.

Beacon Academy. The Next Morning.
--AND WE MADE LIKE HAY AND BAILED, AND I WALKED BLAKE BACK AND SHE JUST--WENT TO BED!
I'M NEVER GONNA FIND A SINGLE THING TO HELP HER WITH! THEY ALL END IN DISASTER!
THAT'S ROUGH. YOU WANT TO COME FEED THE CHICKENS WITH ME? CHICKENS ARE RELAXING.
UGGGGGH.
TAP TAP
WAIT, WAS BLAKE EVEN UPSET?
SHE SAYS SHE'S FINE!
THEN MAYBE YOU SHOULD BELIEVE HER!
I FEEL LIKE IT'S NOT FINE!
THEN YOU SHOULD ASK HER!
WHY ARE YOU BOTH YELLING?!
HOW ABOUT A GOOD SPELL TO BLAST ME FROM THE FACE OF THE EARTH?
ON IT.
YOU KNOW WHAT MAGIC WORDS I THINK YOU'RE FORGETTING, YANG?
NICE TO SEE MY EFFORTS AT A CALAMITOUS SELF-EXCORIATION SPELL WENT UNAPPRECIATED!

BLAKE!
OH, BLAKE--
--I'M SORRY.
I SHOULD HAVE ASKED WHAT IT WAS YOU WANTED TO DO, SHOULD HAVE LISTENED WHEN YOU SAID YOU DIDN'T NEED MY HELP...
...AND IT WON'T HAPPEN AGAIN. FROM NOW ON I'LL LISTEN TO YOU AND I'LL MEET YOU ON YOUR OWN TERMS. I JUST--
--JUST TELL ME HOW TO MAKE IT RIGHT, AND--
UHH... WHAT'S SO FUNNY?
OH, YANG!
THANK YOU. I APPRECIATE EVERYTHING YOU'VE BEEN DOING. BUT SIT.
YOU DON'T NEED AN EXCUSE LIKE "HELPING ME" TO SPEND TIME WITH ME.
YOU CAN'T FIX EVERYTHING, HELP EVERYTHING, CONTROL HOW EVERYTHING GOES. NOT EVEN WITH THE BEST OF INTENTIONS. THAT'S HORROR, NOT COMEDY.
SO LET'S TRY THIS...
YANG, WHY DON'T YOU TELL ME YOUR FAVORITE BOOK--FUNNY, SCARY, WHATEVER YOU LIKE.
TELL IT TO ME LIKE A STORY.

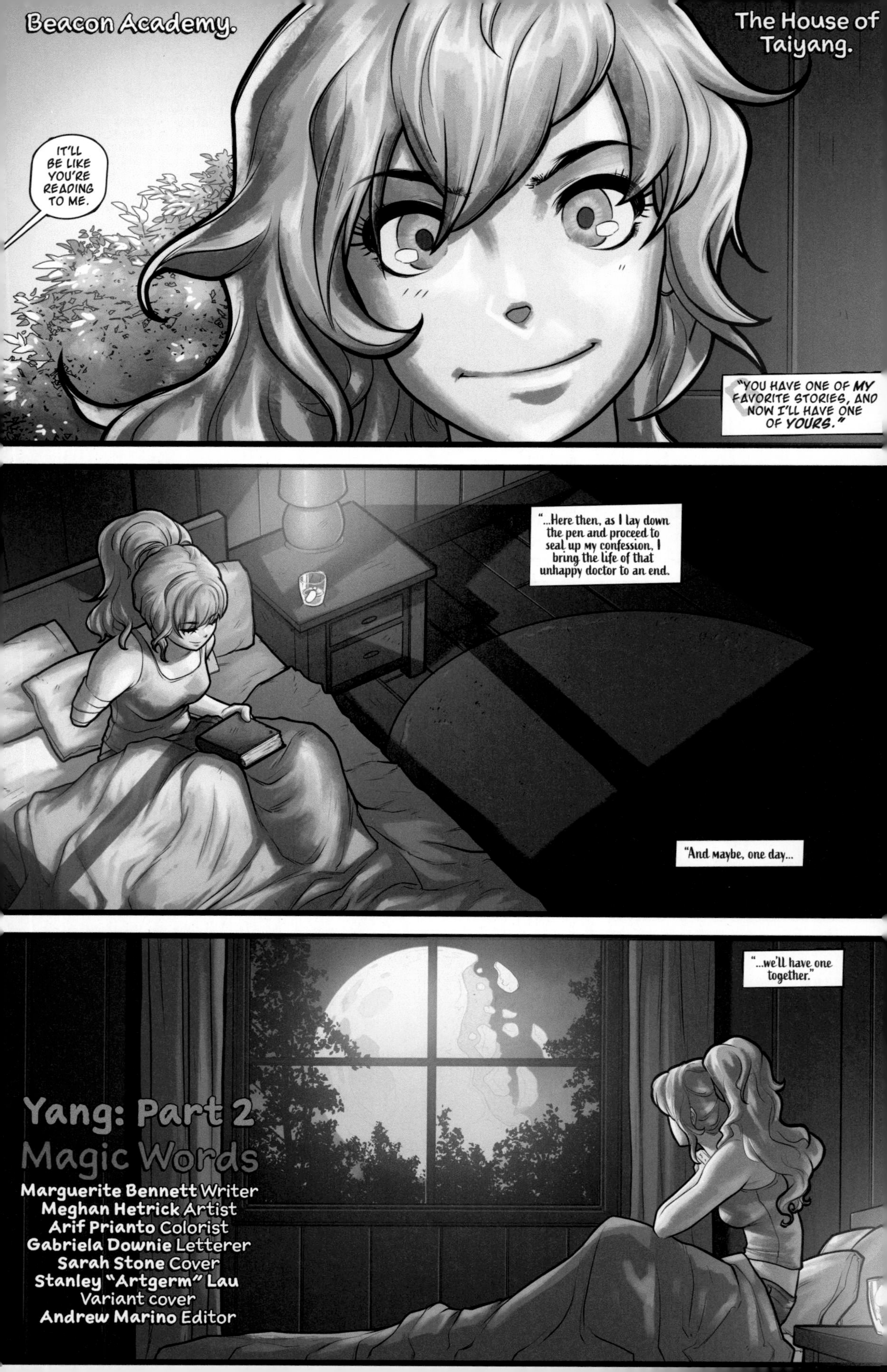

Beacon Academy.
The House of Taiyang.
IT'LL BE LIKE YOU'RE READING TO ME.
"YOU HAVE ONE OF MY FAVORITE STORIES, AND NOW I'LL HAVE ONE OF YOURS."
"...Here then, as I lay down the pen and proceed to seal up my confession, I bring the life of that unhappy doctor to an end.
"And maybe, one day...
"...we'll have one together."
Yang: Part 2
Magic Words
Marguerite Bennett Writer
Meghan Hetrick Artist
Arif Prianto Colorist
Gabriela Downie Letterer
Sarah Stone Cover
Stanley "Artgerm" Lau
Variant cover
Andrew Marino Editor

Menagerie.
I RAN FROM BEACON.
The One That Got Away
Marguerite Bennett Writer
Meghan Hetrick Artist
Arif Prianto Colorist
Gabriela Downie Letterer
Andrew Marino Editor
RAN HOME TO MENAGERIE, TO MY PARENTS' HOUSE, LIKE AN ANIMAL CRAWLING UNDER THE PORCH TO DIE.
BUT THEY DIDN'T LET ME DIE.
The Belladonna House.
THEY DIDN'T TURN ME AWAY FOR BEING A TRAITOR, FOR STAYING WITH THE WHITE FANG AMID THE BLOODSHED, FOR CALLING THEM COWARDS, FOR RUNNING AWAY TO BEACON.
THEY COULD'VE SCREAMED AT ME, SHOUTED AT ME, TOLD ME HOW DISAPPOINTED THEY WERE IN ME, TOLD ME I'D BROUGHT THIS ALL ON MYSELF...
...BUT THEY DIDN'T.
THEY FORGAVE ME.
NO QUESTIONS ASKED, NO DEMANDS MADE.
AND THEY TOOK ME BACK IN.
ONE DAY, I WANT TO BE THE KIND OF PERSON WHO DESERVES MY FRIENDS.
ONE DAY, I WANT TO BE THE KIND OF DAUGHTER WHO DESERVES MY PARENTS.

The Guest Room.
Morning.
MY FATHER BROUGHT DOWN AN OLD TRUNK WITH MY THINGS. DOLLS AND TOYS AND BOOKS...THEY LOOK LIKE THEY BELONG TO A COMPLETELY DIFFERENT PERSON.
THIS SHY, SHELTERED, INNOCENT GIRL WHO NEVER DID ANYTHING EVIL-- NEVER GREW UP.
IF I COULD TALK TO HER NOW...
...I'D TELL HER I'M SORRY.
I'M SORRY THAT I'M YOUR FUTURE.
BLAKE, SWEETHEART?
WE'VE KEPT YOUR RETURN QUIET, AS YOU ASKED, BUT THIS IS CAUSE FOR CELEBRATION.
WHAT DO YOU SAY I MAKE SPECKLED TUNA FOR DINNER? YOUR FAVORITE.
OF COURSE, WE HAVE TO GO FISHING FIRST.
WHY DON'T WE GO CATCH SOME OF THE ONES THAT GOT AWAY?

Azure Island.
DID YOU GIVE THAT FUNNY LITTLE BODYGUARD THE DAY OFF?
SUN WUKONG.
WE'RE PROBABLY THE ONLY TWO HUNTSMEN STUDENTS IN MENAGERIE WHO WERE THERE WHEN BEACON FELL...BUT I THINK HE KNOWS I NEED SOME SPACE RIGHT NOW.
AND SPACE AND SUNSHINE AND FRESH AIR YOU SHALL HAVE.
THE FAUNUS HAVE WORKED SO HARD TO MAKE MENAGERIE INTO A BEAUTIFUL PLACE...BUT THIS ISLAND NEVER NEEDED MUCH HELP.
THE BIGGEST, FATTEST TUNA COME HERE TO EAT THE CRABS AND SQUID THAT MAKE THEIR HOMES AROUND THE ROCKS.
THERE WAS ONE THAT ALWAYS EVADED THE LOCALS! THE BIG ONE, THEY CALLED HIM.
NOT VERY CREATIVE, MAYBE--BUT ABSOLUTE ENCYCLOPEDIAS OF STORIES.
THEY TOLD ME ONE STORY ABOUT A FAUNUS PRINCESS WHO CAME HERE.
SHE WAS IN LOVE WITH A HUMAN, A NOBLE YOUTH SHE COULDN'T HAVE.
"SHE GAVE HIM A SACRED RING CARVED FROM A SEASHELL AS A TOKEN OF HER LOVE.
"WHEN A MESSENGER BROUGHT HER THE RING FROM THE BATTLEFIELD WHERE HER TRUE LOVE FELL, SHE CLIMBED THIS MOUNTAIN AND THREW HERSELF INTO THE SEA.
"'SOME SAY SHE DIED OF A BROKEN HEART,' THE OLD ONES WOULD SAY."

"BUT I THINK IT WAS CLOSER TO A BROKEN NECK."
MOM!
WHAT? THAT'S HOW THEY TOLD IT!
SHAKE SHAKE
MOM... I'M NOT IN DANGER OF DOING ANYTHING LIKE THAT OVER ADAM...
WHOEVER SAID I WAS WORRIED ABOUT YOU DOING ANYTHING BECAUSE OF THAT VICIOUS, TREACHEROUS, MURDEROUS FIEND?
BLAKE, I'M WORRIED ABOUT YOU DOING IT BECAUSE OF YOU.
BECAUSE YOU CAN'T FORGIVE YOURSELF.
STILL PINING AWAY WITH GRIEF AFTER THE ONE THAT GOT AWAY--
--THE VISION OF THE GIRL YOU THOUGHT YOU SHOULD HAVE BEEN.

I DON'T UNDERSTAND WHERE THIS IMAGE OF WHO YOU THOUGHT YOU WERE SUPPOSED TO BE CAME FROM.
BUT, BLAKE, THERE IS NO GIRL YOU WERE SUPPOSED TO BE.
THERE IS NO PAST SELF MORE IMPORTANT THAN WHO YOU ARE RIGHT NOW.
MOM...
...I LET EVERYONE DOWN. I RAN OUT ON YOU AND DAD, AND THEN I FOUND THE--THE BEST FRIENDS, RUBY AND WEISS AND--AND YANG--AND I--
--I RAN OUT ON THEM AGAIN!
HOW CAN ANYONE STILL LOVE ME?!
I DON'T DESERVE YOU.
BLAKE, OH, BLAKE...
WHY WOULD YOU SAY THIS? BECAUSE I TRIED TO RAISE YOU TO BE ABLE TO TALK TO ME? TO BE ABLE TO COME TO ME FOR HELP WHEN YOU WERE IN TROUBLE?
AND YOUR FATHER... BUT WE'LL FIND A WAY TO TALK TO YOUR FATHER.
THAT'S THE FUN THING ABOUT PARENTS AND CHILDREN, BLAKE.
NEITHER OF US DESERVE THE OTHER, AND WE DON'T HAVE TO.
THAT ISN'T HOW IT WORKS.
YOU WILL ALWAYS BE LOVED.

IT WAS NEVER SOMETHING ANYONE TOLD ME TO DO. IT WAS JUST--THERE, LIKE THE GROUND BENEATH MY FEET, OR LIKE THE WIND IN THE TREES. SOMETHING IN THE AIR.
KNOWN.
THAT LOVE IS SUPPOSED TO... REDEEM. THAT IF YOU LOVE SOMEONE ENOUGH, IT WILL FREE THEM.
AND THAT WHETHER YOU'RE FRIENDS OR FAMILY OR ANYTHING MORE--
--GIRLS ARE SUPPOSED TO DO THAT FOR BOYS.
RESCUE THEM.
GENTLE THEM. CIVILIZE THEM.
SAVE THEM.
EVEN IF IT KILLS YOU.
BLAKE, YOU WERE SO YOUNG.
IT WAS OUR JOB AS PARENTS TO PROTECT YOU.
WHATEVER YOU THINK OF WHAT YOU WERE MIXED UP IN, CAN YOU THINK FOR A MOMENT ABOUT HOW WE FELT?
DISAPPOINTED IN ME?
NEVER!
BLAKE, WE WEREN'T ANGRY WITH YOU--WE WERE FURIOUS WITH OURSELVES THAT WE DIDN'T PROTECT YOU FROM HIM!
WE WORKED WITH THE WHITE FANG--AIDED THEM, DEFENDED THEM--RIGHT UNTIL THE MOMENT THEY TURNED TO MURDER TO MEET THEIR ENDS!
ONCE WE REALIZED WHAT HAD BEEN HAPPENING UNDER OUR NOSES--

"-SIGH- IT'S A SIN OF GROWING OLDER, FORGETTING WHAT IT'S LIKE TO BE SO YOUNG.
"WE DIDN'T CREDIT YOU WITH BEING CLEVER ENOUGH TO OUTSMART US, SNEAKING OUT OF THE CAMPS ON THOSE RAIDS WITH THE WHITE FANG.
"AND WE DIDN'T CREDIT ADAM TAURUS WITH BEING SO MISGUIDED AND BRUTAL.
"WE GAVE HIM THE SAME ENDLESS CHANCES, DIDN'T WANT TO 'RUIN HIS FUTURE,' AND THE FUTURE OF ALL THE FAUNUS.
"ONE MUST NOT BE DECEIVED BY APPEARANCES.
"BUT THERE IS NO DECEIT IN ACTIONS--AND WHAT ADAM TAURUS CHOSE TO DO WITH HIS LIFE IS WHAT DEFINES HIM."
IT SCARED ME SO MUCH THAT ONE THING I COULD DO WOULD JUST... RUIN ME IN YOUR EYES.
BLAKE, IF YOU DID SOMETHING SO TRULY UNFORGIVABLE, I WOULD ASK YOU TO FACE JUSTICE-- BUT NEVER WITHOUT STANDING AT YOUR SIDE, NEVER WITHOUT LOVING YOU--
--BECAUSE RESPONSIBILITY IS PART OF LOVE.
BUT, DARLING... YOU WERE AS MUCH ADAM'S TARGET AS ANY OF THE HUMANS HE ATTACKED.
YOU ARE MY CHILD.
THERE IS NOTHING-- NO KINGDOM, NO CAUSE--THAT YOUR FATHER AND I LOVE MORE THAN YOU.
AND YOU CAN GO TO HIM. HE'S BEEN WAITING FOR YOU AS LONG AS I HAVE.
BECAUSE WE WILL ALWAYS BE THERE FOR YOU.
YOU CAN TALK TO US. YOU CAN TELL US ANYTHING.
OR EVEN JUST BE WITH US, AND SAY NOTHING AT ALL.

SPLASH
GASP
THE BIG ONE.

The Belladonna House.
!
THE BOTTLE CAP...?
NO...
THE ONE...
...THAT CAME BACK.
NEXT:
The Hunter or the Hunted?

Schnee Manor.
THIS BOOK IS GOING TO BE THE END OF ME.
I CAN'T MAKE ANY SENSE OF THE BOOK I WON FROM PROFESSOR OZPIN...
IS IT ALL IN CODE? OR A DEAD LANGUAGE?
IT'S A PATTERN I CAN'T DECIPHER, LET ALONE BREAK...
SIGH
WEISS, SWEETHEART...
I'M SO... RELIEVED... TO SEE OUR CONVERSATION AT YOUR DOOR HAS YOU FEELING...A BIT BETTER--
YES. THANK YOU...
...MOTHER.
The Hind
Marguerite Bennett Writer
Meghan Hetrick Artist
Arif Prianto Colorist
Gabriela Downie Letterer
Sarah Stone Cover
Stanley "Artgerm" Lau
Variant Cover
Andrew Marino Editor

COME NOW, SWEETHEART... SIT DOWN...
I'M... ALLOWED IN YOUR GARDEN?
WHY NOT...? YOUR FATHER AND SISTER ARE AWAY...WHO ELSE IS THERE? WHITLEY...?
SPEAKING OF, SWEETHEART, ARE YOU OLD ENOUGH TO DRINK YET? I'M AFRAID...I'VE FORGOTTEN--
WATER WOULD BE LOVELY, KLEIN.
WHERE ARE FATHER AND WINTER, MOTHER?
OH...I DON'T KNOW. THEY'VE GOT SUCH IMPORTANT BUSINESS TO MANAGE.
I'VE NEVER BEEN ABLE TO KEEP UP WITH THEM.
I THINK YOUR FATHER HAS GONE TO MANAGE SOMETHING TO DO WITH THE LATEST BATCH OF FAUNUS WORKERS FOR THE SCHNEE DUST MINES...
...I WOULD BE NOTHING BUT A BURDEN DOWN THERE.

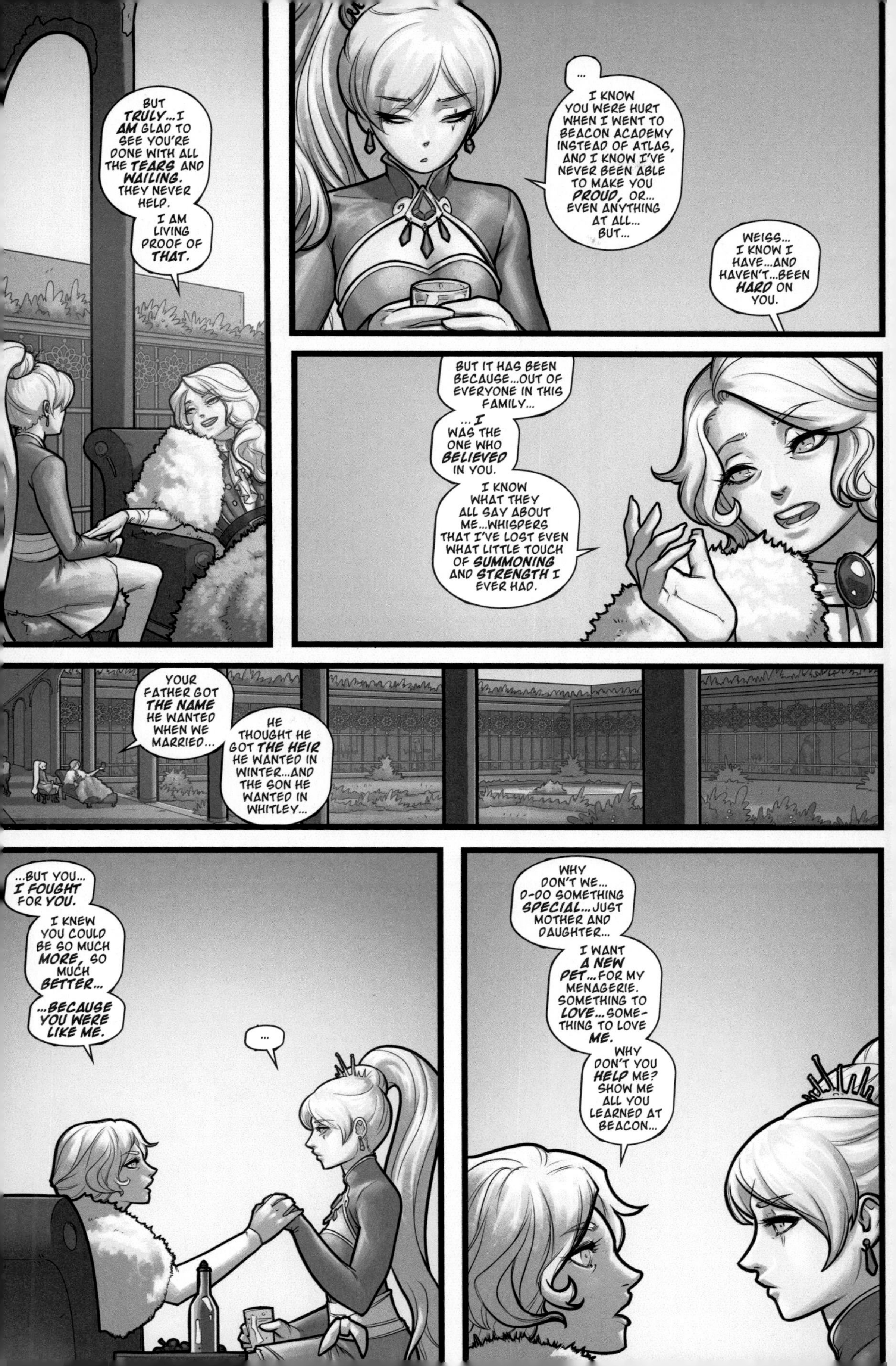

BUT TRULY...I AM GLAD TO SEE YOU'RE DONE WITH ALL THE TEARS AND WAILING. THEY NEVER HELP.
I AM LIVING PROOF OF THAT.
...
I KNOW YOU WERE HURT WHEN I WENT TO BEACON ACADEMY INSTEAD OF ATLAS, AND I KNOW I'VE NEVER BEEN ABLE TO MAKE YOU PROUD, OR... EVEN ANYTHING AT ALL... BUT...
WEISS... I KNOW I HAVE...AND HAVEN'T...BEEN HARD ON YOU.
BUT IT HAS BEEN BECAUSE...OUT OF EVERYONE IN THIS FAMILY...
... I WAS THE ONE WHO BELIEVED IN YOU.
I KNOW WHAT THEY ALL SAY ABOUT ME...WHISPERS THAT I'VE LOST EVEN WHAT LITTLE TOUCH OF SUMMONING AND STRENGTH I EVER HAD.
YOUR FATHER GOT THE NAME HE WANTED WHEN WE MARRIED...
HE THOUGHT HE GOT THE HEIR HE WANTED IN WINTER...AND THE SON HE WANTED IN WHITLEY...
...BUT YOU... I FOUGHT FOR YOU.
I KNEW YOU COULD BE SO MUCH MORE, SO MUCH BETTER...
...BECAUSE YOU WERE LIKE ME.
...
WHY DON'T WE... D-DO SOMETHING SPECIAL...JUST MOTHER AND DAUGHTER...
I WANT A NEW PET...FOR MY MENAGERIE. SOMETHING TO LOVE...SOME-THING TO LOVE ME.
WHY DON'T YOU HELP ME? SHOW ME ALL YOU LEARNED AT BEACON...

"...SHOW ME WHAT MY DAUGHTER CAN DO."
The Snowbound Forest.
THERE IT IS--THE HAILSTONE HIND!
MADAME SCHNEE, PLEASE...
...YOU HAVE NOT RIDDEN IN YEARS!
PERHAPS SOME FOOD, SOME WATER, SOME REST--
I DON'T--NEED REST, KLEIN!
I'M NOT--BROKEN! I CAN STILL--DO THIS!
GO, WEISS!
"PLEASE, BRING IT TO ME..."

WELL DONE, WEISS, DARLING!
THIS IS-- EXHILARATING! I FEEL...SO ALIVE AGAIN!
YES! DO IT, WEISS!
MAKE ME PROUD!
WEISS--!
DARLING!

KLANG
I... I DID IT...
OH, WEISS, SWEETHEART... I KNEW YOU COULD...
HOW ALIVE YOU LOOKED... WHO COULD RESIST YOU, LET ALONE ABANDON YOU?
OH, PLEASE... BIND THE CREATURE AT ONCE, KLEIN.
I KNOW JACQUES WON'T LET ME... KEEP A PET... WITHOUT MAKING SOME SORT OF GALA ABOUT IT.
LET THE USUAL VULTURES COME...COME AND SEE THE SCHNEES' NEWEST CONQUEST.

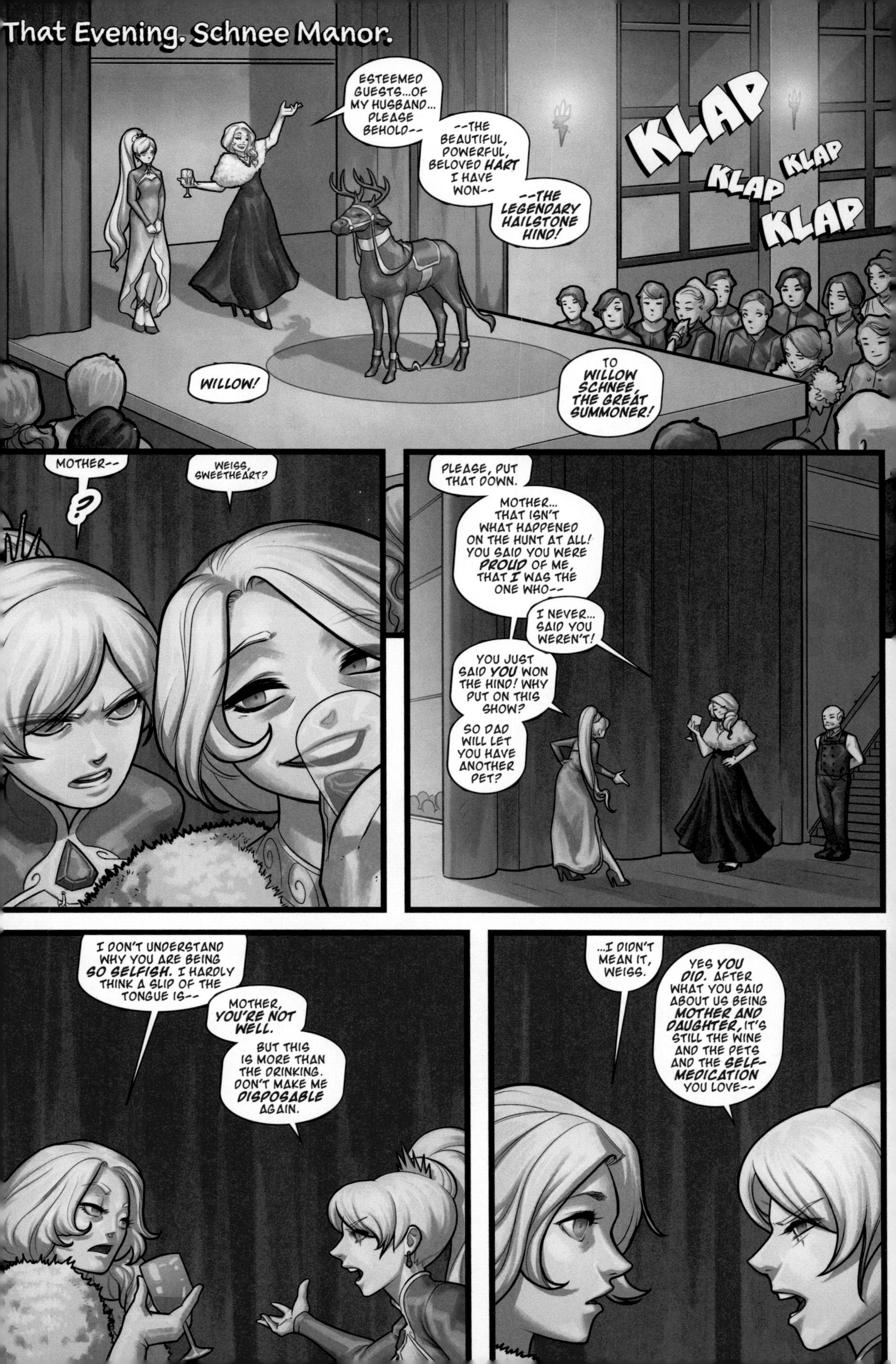
That Evening. Schnee Manor.
ESTEEMED GUESTS...OF MY HUSBAND... PLEASE BEHOLD--
--THE BEAUTIFUL, POWERFUL, BELOVED HART I HAVE WON--
--THE LEGENDARY HAILSTONE HIND!
KLAP
KLAP
KLAP
KLAP
WILLOW!
TO WILLOW SCHNEE, THE GREAT SUMMONER!
MOTHER--
?
WEISS, SWEETHEART?
PLEASE, PUT THAT DOWN.
MOTHER... THAT ISN'T WHAT HAPPENED ON THE HUNT AT ALL! YOU SAID YOU WERE PROUD OF ME, THAT I WAS THE ONE WHO--
I NEVER... SAID YOU WEREN'T!
YOU JUST SAID YOU WON THE HIND! WHY PUT ON THIS SHOW?
SO DAD WILL LET YOU HAVE ANOTHER PET?
I DON'T UNDERSTAND WHY YOU ARE BEING SO SELFISH. I HARDLY THINK A SLIP OF THE TONGUE IS--
MOTHER, YOU'RE NOT WELL.
BUT THIS IS MORE THAN THE DRINKING. DON'T MAKE ME DISPOSABLE AGAIN.
...I DIDN'T MEAN IT, WEISS.
YES YOU DID. AFTER WHAT YOU SAID ABOUT US BEING MOTHER AND DAUGHTER, IT'S STILL THE WINE AND THE PETS AND THE SELF-MEDICATION YOU LOVE--

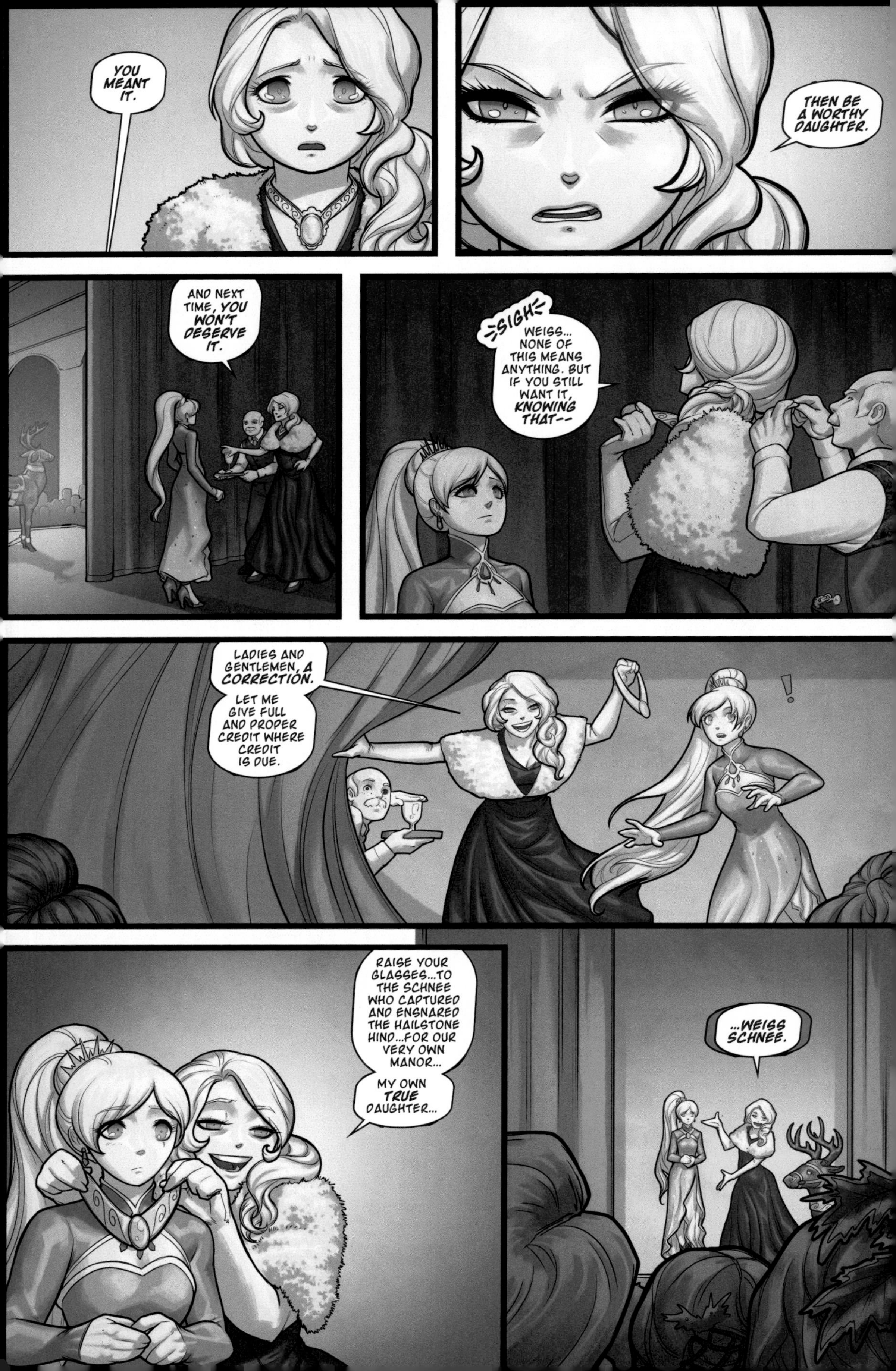
YOU MEANT IT.
THEN BE A WORTHY DAUGHTER.
AND NEXT TIME, YOU WON'T DESERVE IT.
SIGH
WEISS... NONE OF THIS MEANS ANYTHING. BUT IF YOU STILL WANT IT, KNOWING THAT--
LADIES AND GENTLEMEN, A CORRECTION.
LET ME GIVE FULL AND PROPER CREDIT WHERE CREDIT IS DUE.
!
RAISE YOUR GLASSES...TO THE SCHNEE WHO CAPTURED AND ENSNARED THE HAILSTONE HIND...FOR OUR VERY OWN MANOR...
MY OWN TRUE DAUGHTER...
...WEISS SCHNEE.

Midnight.
"WHAT STUNT?"
THAT'S WHAT I SAID TO BLAKE, WHEN SHE SAW WHAT I DID TO CARDIN IN THE OBSTACLE COURSE.
I PRETENDED IT DIDN'T HAPPEN...BUT IT DID.
"WELL, IT WASN'T CHEATING," I TOLD HER. "IT'S NOT MY FAULT IF HE'S STUPID!"
AND IF IT BOTHERED HER, THEN IT WASN'T MY FAULT--I DIDN'T MEAN FOR HIM TO GET HUMILIATED THE WAY HE DID.
AND IF I DID WANT HIM TO GET INTO TROUBLE...
WELL...HE HAD IT COMING, DIDN'T HE?
THE SAME PATTERN, OVER AND OVER AND OVER AND OVER.
NOTHING HAPPENED. AND IF SOMETHING DID, IT WASN'T ALL THAT BAD.
AND IF IT WAS BAD, I DIDN'T CAUSE IT.
AND IF I CAUSED IT, I DIDN'T MEAN FOR IT TO TURN OUT THAT WAY.
AND IF I DID...YOU HAD IT COMING.
MY MOTHER'S OWN TRUE DAUGHTER...
...NOT ANYMORE.

I WANTED TO BE A HUNTRESS.
TO SHOW THE WORLD THAT THIS--WHO AND WHAT AND HOW I AM--IS BECAUSE OF ME, AND ME ALONE.
NOT MY FAMILY.
NOT MY NAME.
I AM ME.
LOOK AT ME, MOTHER.
LOOK AT ME NOW.

The Kingdom of Mistral.
The House of Healing.
MY NAME IS RUBY ROSE.
THESE ARE MY FRIENDS AND TEAMMATES-- JAUNE, REN, AND NORA.
THEY'RE HUNTSMEN, LIKE ME.
The Garden
Marguerite Bennett Writer
Mirka Andolfo Artist
Arif Prianto Colorist
Gabriela Downie Letterer
Andrew Marino Editor
LIKE MY UNCLE QROW.
MY FRIENDS, TEAM RNJR-- WE'VE BEEN TRYING TO GET TO MISTRAL, TO FIND OUT WHY BEACON ACADEMY WAS ATTACKED.
MY UNCLE FOUND US ON OUR JOURNEY, TRIED TO DEFEND US, AND WAS--STRICKEN BY THIS--ASSASSIN WITH A POISON SCORPION TAIL.
PLEASE. CAN YOU HELP HIM?
OF COURSE WE CAN, CHILD.
THIS IS MISTRAL.
YOU'RE SAFE HERE.
YOUR UNCLE IS IN GOOD HANDS.
HE IS RESTING NOW, BUT YOU CAN VISIT HIM IN YOUR ROOMS WHEN YOU ARE READY.

THANK YOU, MADAME XAHN.
YOU LOOK LIKE YOU COULD USE SOMEONE TO TALK TO.
MY FRIENDS... HAVE BEEN THROUGH A LOT.
I THINK THEY NEED SOME TIME TO THEMSELVES RIGHT NOW, AND I DON'T MIND WAITING.
PERHAPS SOME FRESH AIR, FOR CLARITY OF MIND. WHY DON'T YOU TAKE A WALK...
...THROUGH THE GARDEN?
IT LOOKS AWFULLY BIG.
BIG JOURNEYS AND SMALL ALL BEGIN WITH A SINGLE STEP.
WHEN YOU SAY IT LIKE THAT, IT ACTUALLY MAKES IT SOUND A LOT BIGGER, AND ALSO SPOOKY.
HA. WELL...
WATCH OUT FOR THE FLOWERS...
...THEIR PERFUME CAN BE... INTENSE.
BUT WHO KNOWS?

YOU MAY EVEN FIND SOMEONE TO GUIDE YOU.
STILL WALKING, EVEN THOUGH TEAM RNJR MADE IT TO OUR DESTINATION.
LIKE I CAN'T STOP. CAN'T ACCEPT THAT HERE IS WHERE IT ENDS.
BUT THAT'S IT...THAT WAS THE JOURNEY. WE MADE IT TO MISTRAL, DESPITE... EVERYTHING.
UNCLE QROW HURT, JAUNE SO QUIET, REN AND NORA...
...YANG MAY STILL BE MAD AT ME, AND BLAKE AND WEISS...
I MISS THEM SO MUCH.
WHO AM I WITHOUT THEM?
WHEN THERE WAS A TASK, ONE STEP AFTER THE OTHER, ONE FOOT IN FRONT OF THE OTHER, IT DIDN'T HURT AS MUCH.
BUT NOW--
WAITING IS OFTEN HARDEST.
STANDING STILL CAN BE THE WISEST MOVE.
BREATHE.
H-HELLO?
IS SOMEONE THERE?
RUSTLE

...
YOUR SISTER?
WHO SPEAKS?
A RAVEN?
THE SONGBIRD IN THE EGG THAT NEVER HATCHED AT ALL?
!
...YANG?!
YANG--!
YANG, PLEASE--

I CAN'T DO THIS ALONE.
HUNTRESSES... WE'RE NOT SUPPOSED TO BE ALONE.
YOU AND ME... AND ALL OUR FRIENDS...
WE'RE NOT MEANT TO BE ALONE.
OH, CHILD...
YOU ARE NOT ALONE.
NO ONE IS EVERY TRULY ALONE.
I CAN'T LOSE ANOTHER TEAM...
YOU WON'T.
I CAN'T FIGHT THESE BATTLES BY MYSELF!
PERHAPS NOT.
BUT WHAT YOU CAN DO AND WHO YOU ARE-- THESE ARE TWO VERY DIFFERENT THINGS.

FOR YOU TO CONTINUE ON, I WISH YOU TO KNOW THESE THINGS.
FAILURE IS NOT A FAILING.
THE DEAD ARE NOT ALWAYS GONE.
OKAY, WELL...
...ONE OF THOSE IS SELF-CONTRADICTORY, TWO OF THEM ARE OBVIOUSLY UNTRUE, AND ONE OF THEM SOUNDS LIKE IT WOULD GET YOU IN A LOT OF HOT WATER IN, SAY ENGINEERING OR BRIDGE-BUILDING OR ANYTHING THAT REQUIRES STRUCTURAL INTEGRITY TO, YOU KNOW, NOT DIE.
AND HERE I AM AGAIN... TALKING...TO... A BIRD.
AGAIN.

DO NOT MISTAKE WHAT YIELDS FOR WHAT IS WEAK.
FIRE IS NO ONE'S FRIEND.
YOU GRIEVE, RUBY ROSE, HUNTRESS AND STORYTELLER.
YOU FEAR YOU NEED A QUEST TO KEEP YOU WHOLE.
YOU FEEL YOU NEED YOUR FRIENDS MORE THAN THEY NEED YOU.
THIS IS NOT A FLAW.

IT IS A TERRIBLE THING, TO BE DEFINED BY OTHER PEOPLE.
YOU MISS THEM.
BUT KNOW...YOU ARE NOT INCOMPLETE WITHOUT THEM.
NO PERSON IS LESSER FOR BEING ALONE.
THEY MAY BRING FORTH THE BEST IN YOU--
--BUT THAT BEST STILL BELONGS--
--TO YOU.

I'M NOT BROKEN WITHOUT THE PEOPLE I LOVE.
BUT I CHOOSE THEM.
LIKE THEY CHOSE ME.
OVER, AND OVER, AND OVER.
THEY'RE MY TEAM.
AND I'LL NEVER LOVE THEM ANY LESS.
I HAVE SOMETHING I WANT YOU TO KNOW, LITTLE BIRD--
SOMETIMES, THE WAY OUT--

--IS THROUGH.
WHERE... AM...?
OH?
OH MY GOSH!
HEY, YOU FORGOT YOUR--!!
IT'S JUST A LITTLE RED STONE...OR MAYBE A PIECE OF OLD SEA GLASS?
...
WHAT HAVE I BEEN DOING OUT HERE...?
RUBY ROSE?
YOUR UNCLE IS AWAKE...
...YOU'RE THE ONE HE'S ASKING FOR.
Next: A Quest for Answers!

The House of Madame Mallari. The Island of Patch.
YOUR RECUPERATION IS CONSIDERED COMPLETE?
YEAH...AND NOW I'VE GOT WORK TO DO, A LONG WAY AWAY.
SAID MY GOODBYES TO MY DAD THIS MORNING.
WANTED TO SAY THEM TO YOU.
IT WILL ALWAYS BE A JOURNEY, YANG. IT IS NEVER A CHORE DONE, A TASK COMPLETED.
YOU HAVE A RIGHT TO YOUR ANGER AND TRAUMA, BUT NOT A RIGHT TO SURRENDER THE BATTLE AGAINST YOURSELF.
"AND THOUGH IT HAS NEVER BEEN FAIR, YOU ARE AND WILL ALWAYS HAVE TO BE--"
"--YOUR OWN BEST HEALER."
HERE. TO HELP ALONG THE WAY.
"PHYSICIAN, HEAL THYSELF"?
OR TO FLAVOR YOUR COOKING, WHICH YOUR FATHER TELLS ME IS WORSE THAN YOUR BARK.
THANK YOU FOR TODAY, MADAME MALLARI. THANK YOU FOR EVERYTHING.

THE TRUTH IS...I DON'T KNOW IF I'M READY.
I'VE BEEN WORKING, READING, HEALING, LEARNING TO FIGHT AGAIN...
...AND WHAT I'VE LEARNED FROM MY DAD IS THAT MY MOM...
...MY BIRTH MOM, RAVEN, WHO ABANDONED ME AND MY DAD BEFORE SUMMER ROSE LOVED HIM, BEFORE RUBY WAS EVER BORN.
MY MOM CAN GET ME TO RUBY.
BAR
OPEN
IT'D BE REAL EASY TO SAY, "I'VE HAD A LONG DAY. I SHOULD STOP. I DESERVE IT."
BUT I NEED TO FIND MY SISTER, AND MY MOM, AND ALL THE ANSWERS TO QUESTIONS I NEVER GOT THE CHANCE TO ASK
IT'D BE REAL EASY TO SAY, "THOSE PEOPLE NEED MY HELP."
BUT A GOOD DEED THAT'S A DISTRACTION IS STILL A DISTRACTION, ESPECIALLY IF YOU'RE ONLY DOING IT TO AVOID THE REAL WORK AT HAND.
I HAVE A MISSION. I PROMISED I'D BE A BETTER SISTER, AND FRIEND, AND PERSON.
I PROMISED I'D LEARN.
LESSONS ARE ONLY WORDS UNLESS THEY'RE LIVED.
LESSONS ARE ONLY WORDS UNTIL THEY'RE ACTIONS.
AND SINCE THAT'S THE SPIRIT...

...LET'S HAVE A LITTLE ACTION.
OH HO HO, UNWITTING TRAVELER! YOU HAVE ENTERED THE TERRITORY OF THE PICOTEE PIRATES!
SURRENDER YOUR TREASURES, TRESPASSER.
"SURRENDER"--
--ISN'T IN MY VOCABULARY.

PLEASE!
PLEASE, I-I DIDN'T MEAN TO--I'M NOT WITH THEM, REALLY! I WAS JUST TRAVELING WITH THEM, THAT WAS ALL--
YEAH, THAT LOOKED A LOT LIKE TRAVELING, WHAT YOU DID BACK THERE.
YOUR FIST, TRAVELING 120 MILES AN HOUR, RIGHT AT MY LEFT EYE SOCKET.
YOU EVER HEARD THE PHRASE "RUN WITH THE HARES AND HUNT WITH THE HOUNDS"?
'CAUSE IN REAL LIFE, YOU GET KNOWN BY THE COMPANY YOU KEEP.
AND YOU EVENTUALLY BECOME THE PEOPLE YOU CHOOSE TO BE WITH.
PLEASE.
A GRIMM-- A GRIMM ATTACKED OUR TOWN A FEW YEARS AGO.
WHAT'S A CRAFTSMAN SUPPOSED TO DO WITH A BUSTED HAND?
NO WORK, NO DATES--
UGGGH!
YOU ARE NOT SERIOUSLY GIVING ME THE "MY DISABILITY IS WHY I'M A BIG JERK" SPEECH RIGHT NOW.
HOW AM I THE JERK WHEN I TRY TO LEVEL WITH YOU AND THIS IS HOW YOU REACT?!
YOU BOZOS TRIED TO BEAT ME UP AND TAKE MY BIKE!
YOU ARE NOT MY RESPONSIBILITY!
I AM IN A BIG HURRY TO GO FISTFIGHT MY MOM, OKAY?
REMEMBER. LIKE WITH BLAKE.
MEET HIM ON HIS OWN TERMS.
WHAT YOU THINK IS HELP FOR ONE PERSON IS HURT FOR ANOTHER.

OKAY. WHAT HAPPENED TO YOU, THAT SUCKS. THAT'S AWFUL AND UNFAIR.
YOU **STILL** DON'T GET TO TAKE FROM SOMEBODY ELSE BECAUSE A GRIMM TOOK SOMETHING FROM YOU.
AND YOU **DEFINITELY** DON'T GET TO MAKE WHAT HAPPENED TO YOU INTO SOME KIND OF, OF--I DON'T KNOW, **LOW-RENT VILLAIN ORIGIN STORY.**
DON'T **TAR** OTHER PEOPLE WITH **THAT** BIG, UGLY BRUSH.
AND LOOK--THERE'S THIS HEALER, IN MY VILLAGE. SHE DIDN'T HAVE TO HELP ME. I WASN'T HER RESPONSIBILITY.
AND SHE DIDN'T DO IT BECAUSE IT WAS EXPECTED OF HER. SHE REACHED OUT TO ME.
AND SHE TOLD ME, "WHETHER YOU HATE IT, REJOICE IN IT, RESENT IT, LEARN WHAT YOU CAN FROM IT, IGNORE IT, BEAR IT, STRUGGLE WITH IT, SUFFER FROM IT...
"...IT BELONGS TO ME, AND NOT TO--
"--YOU."

YOU ABSOLUTE STINKING DEAD HORSESHOE CRAB THAT WASHED UP AT LOW TIDE.
THERE WAS NOTHING DIFFERENT ABOUT YOUR HAND.
WELL...
...I WOULDN'T QUITE SAY THAT.
ELECTRICALLY CHARGED GLOVES ASIDE--
--MY HAND SURE GOT YOU TALKING, DIDN'T IT?
I KNEW IT WOULD!
YOU'RE ALL THE SAME!
YOU LOVE ACTING ALL BIG AND SILENT AND BETTER-THAN-YOU, BUT YOU'RE ALL BURSTING TO TALK ABOUT HOW BRAVE AND NOBLE YOU ARE FOR TAKING IT ON THE CHIN.
AHHHH!
YOU THINK YOU'RE SO MUCH STRONGER THAN EVERYONE BECAUSE YOU'RE SUFFERING WITH DIGNITY.

ABSOLUTE MARTYR, HERE TO TEACH ME ALL ABOUT PIETY IN THE FACE OF POVERTY.
YOU GET ONE BOO-BOO AND THEN START BLUBBERING ABOUT WHATEVER SURROGATE MOM--
WHAM
RUBBER WHEEL MEANS I CAN LAY HANDS ON BUMBLEBEE, WHETHER OR NOT YOU GOT THOSE ELECTRIC MITTS--
KZZZZZT
--AND YOU'RE GONNA KEEP THEM OFF MY BIKE.
KOFF-KOFF KOFF
M-MERCY...

CARING ABOUT OTHER PEOPLE ISN'T A WEAKNESS.
IT WASN'T MADAME MALLARI'S.
IT ISN'T MINE.
YOUR WEAKNESS IS ASSUMING BODIES DEFINE WORTH.
YOUR WEAKNESS IS THAT YOU'VE LIVED ON THIS PLANET FOR ALL THESE YEARS, AND THIS MEAN, NASTY, SELFISH LITTLE LIFE IS ALL YOU HAVE TO SHOW FOR IT.
BUT ONE DAY SOMEONE ELSE MIGHT CARE ABOUT YOU.
MIGHT TRY TO TEACH YOU A KINDER LESSON.
AND WHO KNOWS? YOU MIGHT EVEN LEARN SOMETHING.
AFTER ALL...
...IT'S A JOURNEY.
NOW...

...RUN.
CAPTAIN! WE, WE W-WAITED FOR YOU--
YOU'RE NOT HURT, MR. CAPTAIN, SIR?
HE HAD HIS WEAPON DESTROYED-- DISARMED EVEN THE CAPTAIN, SHE DID--
YOUR, UM, ORDERS, UH, YOUR ORDERS, O CAPTAIN, SIR?
THE GIRL IS TO HAVE NO TROUBLE FROM THE COAST, DO YOU UNDERSTAND?
NO OTHER PIRATE OR BANDIT OR THIEF OR SOLDIER IS TO ACCOST HER.
SHE'S HARD MEDICINE.

OF A CURE.
The Harbor of Patch.
I'M ON MY WAY, BABY SISTER. NO MORE DISTRACTIONS.
NO FEARS THAT I'M NOT READY. NO FEARS THAT I DON'T KNOW WHAT I NEED.
MAGIC WORDS, RIGHT?
I'M ON MY WAY-- FOR YOU, AND FOR ALL OUR FRIENDS.
I'M ON MY WAY.
I PROMISE.
The Journey
Marguerite Bennett Writer
Mirka Andolfo Pencils
Gabriele Bagnoli Inks
Arif Prianto Colorist
Gabriela Downie Letterer
Sarah Stone Cover
Ejikure Variant Cover
Andrew Marino Editor

Outside of Menagerie.
SINCE COMING HOME TO MENAGERIE, I'VE GOTTEN SOME STUFF STRAIGHT.
LET A FEW THINGS OUT. LET A FEW PEOPLE IN.
HWARR-HISSS!
ONE OF THEM IS ANOTHER SURVIVOR OF BEACON--A HUNTSMAN-IN-TRAINING AND STOWAWAY ON THE SHIP THAT BROUGHT ME HERE.
MY DAD DOESN'T LIKE HIM.
MY MOTHER, ON THE OTHER HAND--
SUN WUKONG AND BLAKE BELLADONNA TO THE RESCUE!
OR, YOU KNOW, BLAKE AND SUN. THAT WORKS TOO.
RUNAWAY HUNTSMEN IN TRAINING ON PATROL!
The Rose
Marguerite Bennett Writer
Mirka Andolfo Pencils
Gabriele Bagnoli Inks
Arif Prianto Colorist
Gabriela Downie Letterer
Andrew Marino Editor

WE'VE GOT YOU! WE'RE THE ONLY HELP FOR MILES.
THE GRIMM ATTACKS ALONG THE COAST HAVE GOTTEN WORSE.
GHIRA BELLADONNA IS URGING PEOPLE TO CENTRALIZE INTO MENAGERIE, AND WE'RE HERE TO ESCORT YOU.
IT'S JUST FOR A LITTLE WHILE, UNTIL WE GET THIS AREA UNDER CONTROL.
YOU SMASHED THAT GRIMM LIKE WOW!
LIKE, HIS FACE, HIS WHOLE FACE CAME OFF!
CLEMENTINE
JUST THE FACEPLATE-- LIKE A MASK--
LIKE A WHITE FANG MASK!
THE-- WHITE FANG?
YEAH! WE HATE THE WHITE FANG!
ADAM TAURUS KILLED OUR UNCLE JETT IN A BIG RAID ON A DUST MINE.
A...A RAID ON A DUST MINE?
WH-WHEN WAS THIS?
"TWO YEARS AGO, IN THE HARBOR OF HAVEN!"
BANG

BLAKE, WHAT'S WRONG?
THE FAMILY. IN THE WAGON. SUN, I--
WHEN I WAS STILL WITH THE WHITE FANG... ADAM TAURUS LED A RAID AND...
SUN, I THINK THIS IS THE FAMILY OF A GUARD ADAM... SHOT.
MAYBE KILLED.
OH BANANAS.
BLAKE, IF YOU WANT TO BAIL, I GOT THIS.
LIKE, YOU CAN SNEAK OUT BEFORE MRS. CLEMENTINE NOTICES--
I CAN'T.
I CAN'T RUN AGAIN.
BLAKE, IF SHE FINDS OUT...
SHE HAS THE RIGHT TO FIND OUT.
PLEASE, BLAKE. DON'T BUY TROUBLE YOU DON'T NEED RIGHT NOW.
WE ARE IN HOSTILE TERRITORY WITH A VILLAGE FULL OF REFUGEES.
IF THE CROWD CATCHES WIND OF THIS, THE SPIKE IN THEIR EMOTIONS WILL DRAW OUT EVERY GRIMM IN THIS FOREST FASTER THAN FRESH-BAKED COOKIES DRAW RUBY!
BUT MAYBE 'S OKAY! MAYBE, UH, MAYBE MRS. LEMENTINE HATED HER BROTHER. MAYBE HE WAS A DISGRACE TO THE FAMILY AND--
SUN.
BLAKE, PLEASE, JUST DO THIS ONE THING FOR ME...

"...NOT YET."
WAIT UNTIL WE'RE BACK IN MENAGERIE, SUN MEANS.
WAIT UNTIL THE WHITE FANG ARE DEFEATED...
WAIT UNTIL YOU'RE 85 AND SHE'S 110 AND YOU'RE SHOOTING SPITBALLS AT EACH OTHER IN THE SAME OLD FOLKS' HOME, BUT PLEASE--
--NOT NOW.
THE ONES WHO GOT AWAY.
THE ONES WHO CAME BACK.
AND THE ONES...
...WHO CAN NEVER COME HOME AGAIN.
YOU CAN HOPE TO FORGIVE YOURSELF.
YOU CAN SEEK TO BE FORGIVEN BY YOUR LOVED ONES.
BUT THE MOST CRUCIAL STEP IN THIS JOURNEY IS STILL THE MOST OBVIOUS AND THE MOST DIFFICULT-

THE FORGIVENESS OF THOSE YOU WRONGED.
YES?
MRS. UH... CLEMENTINE?
HERE, BLAKE.
WE'VE JUST MADE DINNER.
DON'T BE RUDE.
MAY I--
HM. MAY I...SPEAK WITH YOU? A-ALONE?
THANK YOU, MRS. CLEMENTINE, I...
I NEED TO...TO TELL YOU...
I WAS WITH ADAM TAURUS--
--THE NIGHT HE SHOT MY BROTHER.
YES.
I KNOW.

YOU CAME TO MY HOME, WHAT LITTLE SCRAP OF A HOME A CARAVAN IS.
ENJOYED MY HOSPITALITY. ALL THE WHILE, KNOWING.
I COULD HAVE POISONED YOU.
BUT STILL...YOU CAME.
YOU HAD A RIGHT-- --HAVE A RIGHT...
...TO YOUR REVENGE.
AND IF I DEMAND MY REVENGE, RIGHT NOW?
DRAG YOU OUTSIDE, AND TELL ALL MY PEOPLE THAT HERE STANDS MY BROTHER JETT'S MURDERER?
THEN I... I WOULD ASK WHAT YOU REQUIRED OF ME.
TO BELIEVE HOW COMPLETELY, HOW UTTERLY I REGRET THE PAIN HE WAS CAUSED. THE LOSS.
AND IF I ASKED YOU TO DIE? TO PAY FOR HIS LIFE WITH YOURS?
THEN...
...I WOULDN'T BELIEVE YOU EVER LOVED HIM.

WHAT?!
YOU DARE--
IF I-I OFFER YOU...
...THE DAYS... AND THE HOURS OF MY LIFE...
...TO USE THEM TO DO SOMETHING G-GOOD, T-TO-- ATONE...
...AND ALL YOU ASKED FOR WAS...MORE DEATH, MORE SUFFERING, MORE PAIN...
...THAT SEEMS LIKE A VERY UGLY WAY TO REMEMBER HIM.
THAT SEEMS LIKE A VERY UGLY WAY TO PAY THE PRICE OF HIS LIFE.
AND NOT...
...NOT LIKE LOVE AT ALL.
YOU SHOULD HAVE BEEN MORE AFRAID TO COME HERE, BLAKE BELLADONNA.
I KNOW.
NOTHING I TELL YOU WILL CONVINCE YOU OF THE DEPTH OF MY REMORSE. OF MY--DISGUST FOR THE PERSON I WAS.
HOW MUCH I HAVE HATED MYSELF.
HOW MUCH I HAVE WANTED OTHERS TO HATE ME.
OR HOW MUCH I HAVE TRIED TO DO GOOD WITH MY LIFE IN THE DAYS SINCE I LEFT ADAM.

MY BROTHER... DIDN'T DIE THAT NIGHT.
HE CAME HOME. HEALED. DRANK. SNARLED AT THE CHILDREN.
SWORE ABOUT THE WHITE FANG. SWORE ABOUT THE HUMANS WHO HAD USED HIM AND ABANDONED HIM.
HE WAS STILL A FAUNUS, YOU KNOW.
THE S.D.C.* HIRED HIM AS A GUARD, AS LIVING PROOF THAT THEY DIDN'T THINK WE WERE ALL VERMIN...
...ALL WHILE USING OUR LABOR IN THOSE MINES.
HE WAS DRINKING AND SNARLING AND SWEARING ABOUT ADAM TAURUS THAT NIGHT.
FELL FROM THE BRIDGE WHERE HE WAS WALKING.
*THE SCNEE DUST COMPANY! --ANDREW
DIED OF A BROKEN HEART.
OR A BROKEN NECK.
IT WAS ADAM TAURUS WHO KILLED HIM. BUT IT WASN'T ADAM TAURUS ALONE.
WE BEGGED JETT NOT TO GO AND WORK FOR THE VERY PEOPLE EXPLOITING AND ABUSING US. BEGGED HIM NOT TO DO THIS, FOR MONEY.
BUT WE NEVER KNOW HOW STORIES END, AFTER WE LEAVE THEM.
I DON'T KNOW WHAT WOULD HAVE CHANGED.
YOU LEFT OUR STORY.
AND THEN YOU CAME BACK.

YOU CHOSE TO COME BACK.
YOU DIDN'T KNOW WHO WE WERE AT FIRST.
YOU PLAYED WITH THE CHILDREN. SAVED US FROM THE GRIMM.
NOT BECAUSE YOU WANTED FORGIVENESS.
JUST BECAUSE.
AND WHEN YOU LEARNED...
...YOU DIDN'T RUN.
YOU STAYED. YOU CAME TO ME, AND CONFESSED.
OFFERED ME THE LABOR OF YOUR LIFE, IN PAYMENT FOR ALL MY BROTHER COULD HAVE DONE.
MY BROTHER... WAS NOT A GOOD PERSON.
HE WAS RESPONSIBLE FOR THE SUFFERING OF THE WORKERS HE GUARDED. OUR OWN PEOPLE.
BUT HIS DEATH PUT AN END TO ANY HOPE OF CHANGE, OF... REHABILITATION.
THAT'S THE EVIL OF DEATH. THAT NO MORE GOOD CAN COME.
HE MIGHT HAVE BEEN A GOOD PERSON ONE DAY.

AS YOU HAVE BECOME.
ALL THAT'S LEFT OF US IS WHAT WE MADE WITH OUR LIVES.
AND YOU ARE MAKING... SOMETHING GOOD.
COME HERE, BLAKE BELLADONNA.
I FORGIVE YOU.
I AM NOT THE FIRST.
AND I TRULY BELIEVE...
...I WILL NOT BE THE LAST.
Next: Prison Break!

The Schnee Mansion.
THE GLASS BUBBLE. THE GOLDEN CAGE.
THE SNOWFLAKE IN THE STORM.
ONE LAST BREAKOUT.
HEAVY. YOU SURE YOU DON'T NEED HELP?
...I NEED TO GO, KLEIN.
TONIGHT.
NOW.
THE CARGO PILOT I'VE BRIBED WILL WAIT UNTIL JUST BEFORE DAWN. BUT YOU MUST HURRY, MS. SCHNEE.
YOU MUST CHOOSE, ONCE AND FOR ALL, WHAT IT IS YOU WANT.
SKREEE
?
MY MOTHER'S TRUE PRIDE AND JOY...
...HER MENAGERIE.

SHHHH.
I'M HERE TO HELP, BUT I HAVE TO HURRY.
The Cage
Marguerite Bennett - Writer
Mirka Andolfo - Pencils
Gabriele Bagnoli - Inks
Arif Prianto - Colorist
Gabriela Downie - Letterer
Sarah Stone - Cover
Derrick Chew - Variant Cover
Andrew Marino - Editor
DON'T GIVE ME THAT LOOK! YOU'RE TALL, BUT I NEED HEELS--
GOTCHA, AND--
?

COME ON! NO TROUBLE, NOW!
YOU SHOULD BE **GRATEFUL** FOR THIS TREATMENT, AFTER WHERE YOU'VE BEEN--
WE WANT YOU GOOD AND STRONG, DON'T WE--
IF I MISS THE CARGO SHIP...
NO. IT DOESN'T MATTER.
NO MORE HAILSTONE HINDS.
SNEAKING AWAY LIKE A THIEF IN THE DEAD OF NIGHT?

I SHOULD HAVE KNOWN NOT EVEN YOU WOULD STAY BY MY SIDE.
ABANDONED BY WINTER, BY WHITLEY, BY EVEN YOUR FATHER...
I SHOULD'VE SEEN IT COMING, REALLY.
NO MATTER WHAT I GIVE ANY OF YOU, YOU ALL STILL LEAVE ME IN THE END...
MOTHER... THESE FAUNUS, I'M GOING TO SET THEM FREE--
CONVICT LABOR, SWEETHEART... FOR THE DUST MINES.
"IT USED TO BOTHER ME TOO. BUT THEY'RE RABBLE-ROUSERS, POLITICAL PRISONERS, YOU KNOW THE SORT...
"PERFECTLY LEGAL, YOUR FATHER ASSURES ME, A-AND YOUR FATHER...YOUR FATHER KNOWS BEST.
"I'VE LEARNED THAT, TOO."

AS I'VE LEARNED THERE'S NOTHING I'LL EVER BE ABLE TO DO TO MAKE YOU LOVE ME.
BEING THE VICTIM OF A CYCLE DOESN'T EXCUSE YOU FROM TRYING TO BREAK OUT OF IT, MOTHER.
YOU THINK YOU CAN ESCAPE THIS?
HOW CAN YOU JUDGE ME AFTER ALL I'VE HAD TO ENDURE?!
I'M BREAKING THOSE FAUNUS OUT OF THEIR CHAINS. WE HAVE NO RIGHT TO DO TO THESE POOR PEOPLE WHAT FATHER HAS BEEN DOING--
YOU CARE MORE ABOUT STRANGERS THAN YOU DO YOUR OWN MOTHER!
DO YOU HAVE ANY IDEA WHAT HAPPENS TO GIRLS...TO WOMEN...WHO DISOBEY AT SCHNEE MANOR?
I AM SO...
...SORRY FOR YOU.
BUT I AM NOT "YOUR NEWEST CONQUEST."
YOU WANT ME TO STAY, MOTHER?

PROVE IT.
MAKE ME PROUD.

EVERYTHING WE'VE DONE FOR YOU. EVERY ADVANTAGE--
WE'VE BEEN GIVEN TOO MUCH TO STAND ASIDE AND LET EVIL THINGS HAPPEN!
ISN'T THAT WHAT YOU HOPED TO DO WITH OUR FAMILY LEGACY, BEFORE MY FATHER STOLE IT?!
TO BE THE GOOD YOU HOPED TO SEE IN THE WORLD?
AHHHH!

FAUNUS! SEIZE THE SHIP!
DON'T SHOOT MADAME SCHNEE'S PRIZED COLLECTION!
WEISS.
NO ONE BELONGS IN A CAGE, MOTHER.
NOT THE FAUNUS.
NOT YOUR ANIMALS.
NOT ME.
AND NOT YOU.

YOU ARE MY MOTHER.
AND I LOVE YOU.
BECAUSE OF AND DESPITE ALL OF THIS...
...I STILL LOVE YOU.
BUT I CANNOT BE THE NEXT STAGE IN THIS CYCLE.
I CAN'T BE THE NEXT HIND YOU'RE GOING TO HUNT.
AND I CAN'T GROW UP TO BE YOU.

HURT PEOPLE HURT PEOPLE.
BUT THE PATTERN HAS TO END.
THE CAGE HAS TO BE BROKEN...
...AND SO DOES THE CODE.

Mistral. Now.
THIS IS WHERE IT ENDS, BUT ONLY FOR TODAY.
ONE WALKING UNDER THE EARTH.
THIS WILL HELP US UNDERSTAND WHY BEACON WAS ATTACKED, RIGHT?
Anima. Now.
ONE HEADING THROUGH THE FIRE.
WHEREVER YOU ARE, MOM, I'M COMING FOR YOU, AND I'M COMING FOR ANSWERS.
Menagerie. Now.
IT'S OKAY. IT'S TIME TO MAKE AMENDS FOR WHAT I'VE DONE.
ONE WAITING BY THE WATER.
En Route. Now.
ONE FLYING IN THE AIR.
THIS WILL BREAK THE CHAIN... THIS WILL BREAK THE CODE...
AND EVEN THOUGH WE'RE APART, I KEEP THINKING OF WHAT WE'VE LEARNED, AND HAVE YET TO DISCOVER...

Patch. Then.
THOUGH STORIES HOLD POWER, THE TRUTH WILL BRING YOU CLOSER TO HAPPINESS.

Beacon. Then.
CARING FOR OTHERS CAN MEAN MEETING THEM ON THEIR OWN TERMS.

The Headquarters of the White Fang. Now.
TO SOLVE A PROBLEM, YOU MUST FACE IT, AND CALL IT BY ITS TRUE NAME.

Beacon Academy. Then.
ADULTHOOD IS LEARNING TO TAKE RESPONSIBILITY FOR YOUR ACTIONS, THEIR MOTIVES, AND THEIR UNFORESEEN CONSEQUENCES.

The Village. Now.
GROWTH ONLY COMES WITH CHANGE.

The Island of Patch. Now.
YOU HAVE A RIGHT TO YOUR ANGER AND TRAUMA, BUT NOT A RIGHT TO SURRENDER THE BATTLE AGAINST YOURSELF.

Azure Island. Long Ago.
THE PAST IS A GUIDE, AND NOT A PUNISHMENT.
Schnee Manor. Now.
BEING THE VICTIM OF CYCLES OF ABUSE DOESN'T EXCUSE YOU FROM FIGHTING TO BREAK THOSE CYCLES.

The Maze. Then.
THE WAY OUT IS ALWAYS THROUGH.

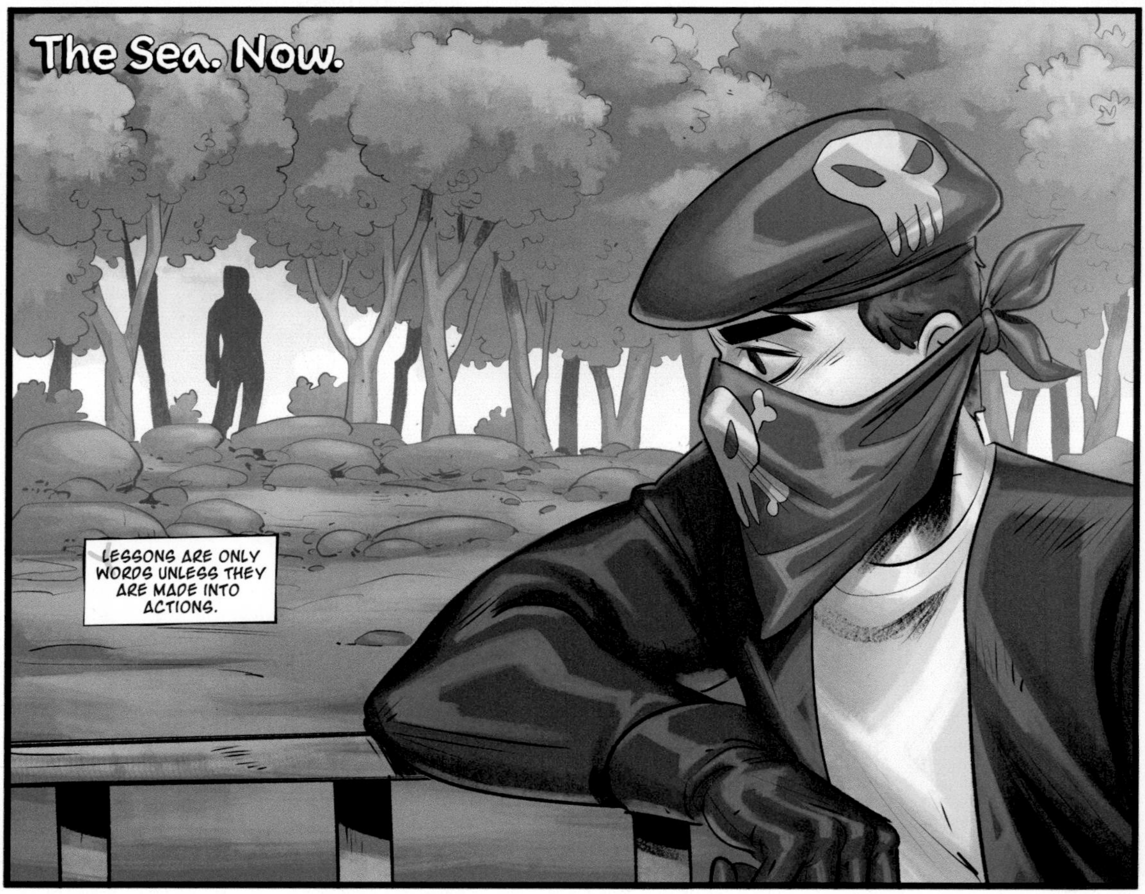
The Sea. Now.
LESSONS ARE ONLY WORDS UNLESS THEY ARE MADE INTO ACTIONS.

The Forest. Now.
YOUR LEGACY WILL BE DEFINED BY WHAT YOU DO WITH THE TIME YOU HAVE.

Schnee Manor. Now.
WILLOW?! WILLOW! YOU WILL OPEN THIS DOOR IF YOU KNOW WHAT'S GOOD FOR YOU, WIFE!
WHAT IS RIGHT MUST BE PLACED ABOVE COMFORT...AND VALIDATION.

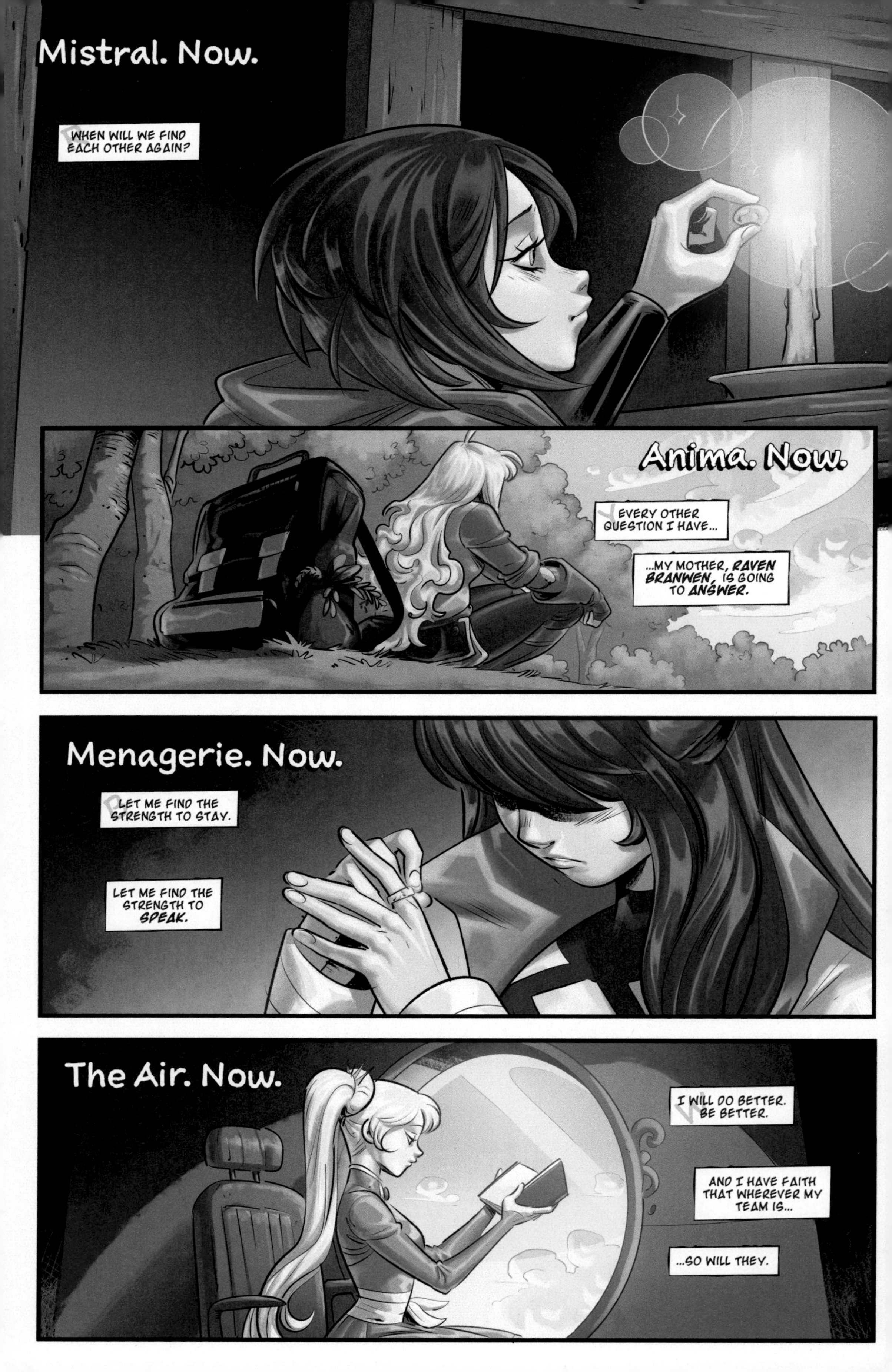
Mistral. Now.
WHEN WILL WE FIND EACH OTHER AGAIN?
Anima. Now.
EVERY OTHER QUESTION I HAVE...
...MY MOTHER, RAVEN BRANWEN, IS GOING TO ANSWER.
Menagerie. Now.
LET ME FIND THE STRENGTH TO STAY.
LET ME FIND THE STRENGTH TO SPEAK.
The Air. Now.
I WILL DO BETTER. BE BETTER.
AND I HAVE FAITH THAT WHEREVER MY TEAM IS...
...SO WILL THEY.

Mistral.
NO MATTER HOW BLEAK, DARK, AND SIGHTLESS THE WORLD BECOMES, WE'RE STILL HERE.
Anima.
LIFE AND BEAUTY AND COLOR AND STORIES ARE STILL HERE.
Menagerie.
WE'LL COME BACK.
The Air.
WE'LL GO ON.

Soon.
WE GO ON--
--TOGETHER.
The Anthem
Marguerite Bennett – Writer
Mirka Andolfo – Pencils
Gabriele Bagnoli – Inks
Arif Prianto – Colors
Gabriela Downie – Letters
Andrew Marino – Editor

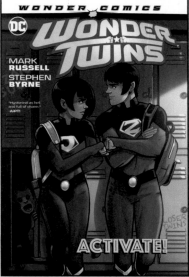

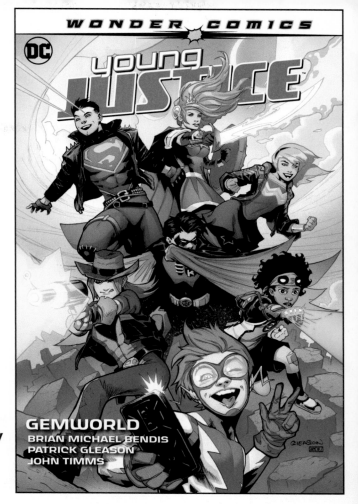

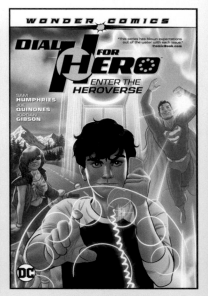

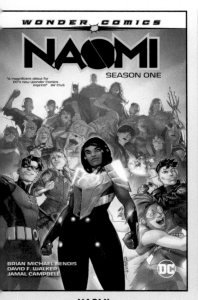

"These are strong, realized women capable of wondrous feats, and Bennett ensures that they remain the heroes of their own stories."
–IGN

"BOMBSHELLS is a win for both female characters and female creators, and that double victory is well worth celebrating."
–NEWSARAMA

DC COMICS
BOMBSHELLS
MARGUERITE BENNETT and MARGUERITE SAUVAGE

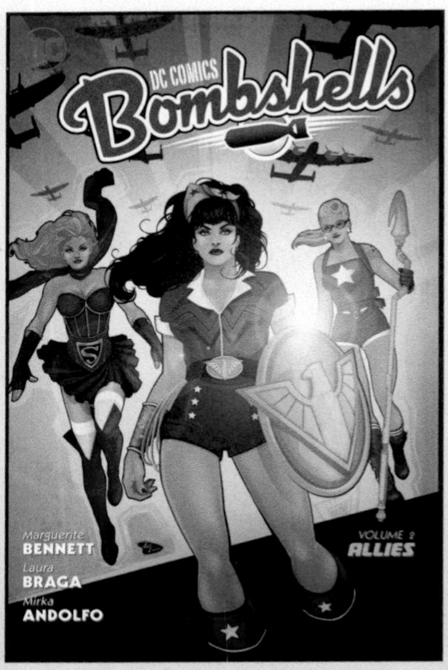

DC COMICS BOMBSHELLS
VOL. 2: ALLIES

DC COMICS BOMBSHELLS
VOL. 3: UPRISING

READ THE ENTIRE EPIC

DC COMICS BOMBSHELLS
VOL. 4: QUEENS

DC COMICS BOMBSHELLS
VOL. 5: THE DEATH OF ILLUSIONS

DC COMICS BOMBSHELLS
VOL. 6: WAR STORIES

Get more DC graphic novels wherever comics and books are sold!